Workbook for
Keys to Teaching Grammar
to English Language Learners

KEITH S. FOLSE, Ph.D.
TESOL Program
University of Central Florida

EKATERINA V. GOUSSAKOVA
English for Academic Purposes Program
Seminole Community College

D1598029

Ann Arbor
University of Michigan Press

♾ Printed on acid-free paper

ISBN-13: 978-0-472-03338-6

2017   2016   2015   6   5   4

CONTENTS

HOW TO USE THIS WORKBOOK

This workbook contains more than 200 exercises to practice the material in *Keys to Teaching Grammar to English Language Learners: A Practical Handbook*. The five chapters in this workbook match the five chapters in the Handbook (HB). The relevant Handbook pages appear after each exercise title as HB pp. 219–223, for example.

Chapter 1 has two parts. Section 1 provides practice differentiating native speaker grammar from ELL grammar. For example, a typical native speaker error might be *Where are you at?* (instead of *Where are you?*), to which an ELL might reply *I'm in home* instead of *I'm at home*. Section 2 helps you see where you are on the grammar continuum. How will gaining knowledge about ELL grammar inform your teaching style?

Chapter 2 deals with native speaker English, including basic grammar labels. Chapter 2 has four sections. Section 1 deals with 20 typical native speaker errors. It is recommended that you dedicate more of your time to the errors that are problematic for you instead of trying to deal with all 20 errors. Section 2 covers the eight parts of speech. These exercises allow you to make the connection between previous grammar training that you may have had as a native speaker and ELL grammar errors. Section 3 has exercises that practice basic sentence labels such as subject, verb, clause, and the like. Finally, Section 4 provides numerous exercises on the 12 verb tenses in English.

Chapter 3 covers 15 grammar points, called Keys, that are basic to teaching English language learners. Keys 1–4 cover verb tenses. Keys 5–15 cover typical ELL grammar issues such as count and non-count nouns, prepositions, and word formation. For each Key, a series of exercises follows that includes understanding definitions, recognizing typical ELL errors for a grammar point, and editing sample student writing. Each Key in the Workbook ends with a small project called Action Research Project to Inform Your Teaching. You are asked to apply your knowledge gained about the Key through a variety of activities, including analyzing excerpts of written English, spoken English, or both to identify how the Key is actually used in real English, or by working with ELLs to translate sentences that practice the Key to consider native language interference in learning the Key.

Chapter 4 consists of 20 "Hot Seat" Questions. It is recommended that you answer each of these questions very early in your coursework. In many cases, you may have no idea what the answer is, but that is exactly where your ELLs are, too, so it is good for you to see these grammar questions from your ELLs' viewpoint.

Chapter 5 deals with various techniques for teaching ELLs. The best way for you to practice these techniques is to see someone using them as you observe his or her classes. Some class observation forms are included here.

Reflecting the variety of content from chapter to chapter, the exercises in each chapter vary in format, number, and length.

Action Research Projects to Inform Your Teaching

After each of the 15 Keys in Chapter 3, an action research project that helps connect grammar information with real-world learning is provided. Each project facilitates understanding why ELLs have difficulty with certain aspects of the grammar in that Key and/or understanding how that grammar is currently used in English.

1

An Introduction to Grammar for English Language Learners (ELLs)

PRACTICE FOR SECTION 1:
What Do You Already Know about ELL Grammar? (Pre-Tests)

Exercise 1.01: Distinguishing Traditional Grammar and ELL Grammar (HB pp. 1–15)

In each of these sentences, underline the grammar error, and then circle NS or ELL to indicate whether the error is more often committed by native speakers or ELLs.

NS	ELL	1. Global warming could to harm our planet forever. We must to act now.
NS	ELL	2. If you would have considered more information, perhaps you would be working in a very different place today.
NS	ELL	3. The meeting began promptly in noon.
NS	ELL	4. Most historians agree that George Washington was great president.
NS	ELL	5. Let's take them boxes to the car now before it rains.
NS	ELL	6. I don't think our decision will effect anyone really.
NS	ELL	7. When did you get married with him?
NS	ELL	8. The most important thing in the life is the friendship.
NS	ELL	9. The program that my company uses today to prevent consumer fraud was invented by Jonathan Spears and myself in 2004.
NS	ELL	10. Turkey is the place that I would like to visit it in the near future.
NS	ELL	11. The police are not sure about when the accident was happened.
NS	ELL	12. If you're not feeling well, then you should lay down for a little while.
NS	ELL	13. He was completely surprised. You should have saw his face.
NS	ELL	14. There are kitten's for sale at that house.

Exercise 1.02: Distinguishing Traditional Grammar and ELL Grammar (HB pp. 1–15)

In each of these sentences, underline the grammar error, and then circle NS or ELL to indicate whether the error is more often committed by native speakers or ELLs.

NS   ELL   1. I wish I had went to your party. I hear it was a huge success.

NS   ELL   2. When I was shave today, I cut myself just above my upper lip.

NS   ELL   3. The best decorated house belongs to the Smiths' without any doubt.

NS   ELL   4. The teacher decided to put off to give us the exam until next week.

NS   ELL   5. Columbus couldn't sail on no more trips because he didn't have money.

NS   ELL   6. The prize will go to whomever has the most points at the end of 20 minutes of play.

NS   ELL   7. Luke won the prize. In every competition, he always has lucky.

NS   ELL   8. Between you and I, there is no reason to rush to finish this project now.

NS   ELL   9. My car is not run well today. I'm not sure what is wrong.

NS   ELL   10. We should of watched the weather report last night to find out the chance of rain for today.

NS   ELL   11. Could you tell me where Jacob lives at?

NS   ELL   12. Swallowtail butterflies can be recognized by their unique colorment.

NS   ELL   13. To complete this task successfully, each of you will need more equipments and supplies.

NS   ELL   14. If you have any extra scraps of material, do not throw away them. Give them to us so they can be recycled.

Exercise 1.03: Answering ELL Grammar Questions (HB pp. 1–15)

Working individually and then with a partner, answer these questions typically asked by ELLs.

1. I know that *another* is singular and *others* is plural, but what about *other*? Is it singular or plural? I can say *my other cat* and *my other cats*, right? What is the rule for these words?

_____

_____

_____

_____

_____

_____

2. Is *had had* correct? Can you say *I had had a headache all day?* What is this verb tense called?

_____

_____

_____

_____

_____

_____

3. How do you form the possessive of nouns in English? I know you use an apostrophe, but when do you put *'s* and when do you put *s'*?

_____

_____

_____

_____

_____

_____

Exercise 1.04: Researching ELL Grammar Questions (HB pp. 1–15)

Observe a grammar (or other subject) ELL class. Write the questions that students ask. If you cannot observe a class, then conduct a virtual interview (via phone, email, listserv, or chat room) with a teacher to find out specific grammar questions that his or her ELLs actually ask during a given lesson.

1. _____

   _____

   _____

2. _____

   _____

   _____

3. _____

   _____

   _____

Exercise 1.05: Identifying ELL Errors in Authentic Material (HB pp. 1–15)

The following excerpt is from an email message that an adult ELL wrote to her teacher, asking for permission for her teenage son to be able to attend her English class with her a few times. Identify and correct the ten errors. Decide how you might explain these errors to this ELL writer.

Dear Teacher,

   Tomorrow start English classes, and I am really excited for that. I have a questions for you. My son has 15 years old, and he is in vacation from school now. He has to return to Brazil in February, and I would like to invite him to our class just for a little days. He speak English, but he needs practice more. I really believe that this classes is just what he needs.

   Is possible for him to attend this class?

                                                        Sincerely,

                                                        Rebeka

---

Exercise 1.06: Identifying ELL Errors in Authentic Material (HB pp. 1–15)

When completing their writing assignments for content classes such as history or literature, some ELLs tend to make more errors than they would in their ELL classes because they are concentrating on the subject information instead of the language. The following excerpt is from an assignment written by an ELL in a world geography class. The assignment was to write about a geographic area that the ELL knew about firsthand or had researched in the library. Unfortunately, this small excerpt has at least 20 errors. The errors are so numerous that they impede the writer's intended message. Identify the errors, and decide how you would explain them to the ELL.

Dominican Republic and Haiti
Dominican Republic is a country located at the Caribbean. This nation share one island with Haiti. both are nations poors, but Dominican Republic have two third of the island, and its natural resources are more accessibles than the Haiti natural resources. The economy in Haiti is not so good, so this make the haitian population to move to Dominican Republic in order to get prosperity. This economic situation force them to cross the frontier and stay iligaly in Dominican Republic, generating a problem similar to the actual ilegal inmigration we have in the Unite State of America.

Exercise 1.07: Action Research: Comparing ELL and Native Speaker Language (HB pp. 1–15)

Give the same short writing assignment to a native speaker and to a non-native speaker. (The two participants should be as similar as possible in characteristics that might affect their language, such as age, level of education, socioeconomic status, etc.) Analyze the two pieces of writing to find any differences in the language used.

Examples of possible writing tasks include:

1. In 100–125 words, describe your ideal house.
2. In 100–125 words, explain how to make your favorite recipe.
3. In 100–125 words, who is the person—dead or alive—that you would most like to interview and why?

Additional Research Question: How would any of these three comparisons be different if students were given a time limit instead of a word limit?

PRACTICE FOR SECTION 2:
Approaches to Teaching ELL Grammar: The Role of Student, Setting, Course, and Teaching Situation

Exercise 1.08: Lesson Plans for Grammar Teaching, the Direct Approach (HB pp. 16–30)

Search the Internet for a lesson plan where grammar is being taught directly. In three to five minutes, give an overview of the lesson plan to your classmates. Which specific grammar points are being covered? Does the plan indicate how the grammar will be presented? How will the grammar be practiced? Is the practice written, spoken, or both?

Exercise 1.09: Lesson Plans for Grammar Teaching, the Indirect Approach: ESP (HB pp. 16–30)

One type of class that often uses an indirect approach to grammar learning is an English for Specific Purposes (ESP) class. Search the Internet for a lesson plan for an ESP course such as business, medical, legal, etc. In three to five minutes, give an overview of the lesson plan to your classmates. Is grammar covered? If so, how? If not, why do you think it is not covered? If the plan includes grammar, does the plan indicate how the grammar will be presented? How will the grammar be practiced? Is the practice written, spoken, or both?

Exercise 1.10: Lesson Plans for Grammar Teaching, the Indirect Approach: Kindergarten (K–2) (HB pp. 16–30)

Songs are a part of all classes for young learners in all countries. Because of the repetition in songs, the lyrics are a good source of English input for ELLs. In fact, a song can be thought of as a language drill set to music. Look at the lyrics to the classic song "Old MacDonald Had a Farm," and then identify the grammar points that ELLs will practice as they sing this song.

"Old MacDonald Had a Farm"	*Grammar Items*
Old MacDonald had a farm, E-I-E-I-O And on his farm he had a cow, E-I-E-I-O With a "moo-moo" here and a "moo-moo" there Here a "moo" there a "moo" Everywhere a "moo-moo" Old MacDonald had a farm, E-I-E-I-O	A. Old MacDonald was male. Put A by the two grammar items that show this. B. The basic sentence pattern in English is Subject-Verb-Object (SVO). Put B by the three examples of this. C. In English, singular count nouns need something in front of them, such as *a, an, the, my, your, his, this,* etc. Put C by the nine examples of this. D. In English, most places are preceded by *at, on,* or *in.* Put D by the prepositional phrase of place. E. The past tense of have is *had,* not **haved.* Put E by the three examples of this.

Exercise 1.11: Lesson Plans for Grammar Teaching, the Indirect Approach: Middle School (HB pp. 16–30)

ELLs learn academic English from their textbooks. Look at this problem posed in a science book, and then identify the grammar items that ELLs will be exposed to as they work to solve the problem.

Science Problem	Grammar Items
A student wants to find out the kind of soil that can hold the most water. She buys four identical pots with small holes in the bottom of each. She then fills each pot with a different kind of soil and waters the pots with the exact same amount of water. How can she determine the amount of water that stays in the soil in each pot? A. By putting cotton in each pot to see how much water it absorbs. B. By carefully examining the growth of flowers in each of the pots. C. By covering only three of the pots with a plastic bag. D. By measuring how much water drains from each pot.	A. In simple present tense, the verb after 3rd person singular ends in –s. Write A by the seven examples of this. B. Modals such as *can, would,* and *will* are followed by the simple form of the verb. Put B by the two examples of this. C. Singular count nouns need something in front of them, such as *a, an, the, my, your, his, this,* etc. Put C by the 11 examples of this. D. In English, a word can sometimes be used as different parts of speech without changing its form. Underline the six usages of any form of the word *water.* Put N by the noun usages and V by the verb usages. E. After a preposition, we use a gerund (*–ing* verb form used as a noun) instead of simple form or the infinitive (*to* + VERB). Put E by the four examples of this. F. Which four non-count nouns are used in this science passage? _____ _____ _____

NOTE: The correct answer to the science problem presented in Exercise 1.11 is D.

Exercise 1.12: Grammar Teaching Settings: Which One Are You? (HB pp. 16–30)

Different types of teachers use ELL grammar knowledge in different ways. To what degree does each of these eight teaching situations apply to your teaching setting? Rank them from 0 (not at all like my teaching situation) to 10 (exactly like my teaching situation).

Teaching Situation	Scale
1. I am an ELL grammar teacher.	← 0—1—2—3—4—5—6—7—8—9—10 →
2. I assess ELLs' writing.	← 0—1—2—3—4—5—6—7—8—9—10 →
3. I judge the readability of texts for ELLs.	← 0—1—2—3—4—5—6—7—8—9—10 →
4. I teach a K–12 subject other than ESL.	← 0—1—2—3—4—5—6—7—8—9—10 →
5. I assess the growth of ELLs' proficiency in English.	← 0—1—2—3—4—5—6—7—8—9—10 →
6. I answer ELLs' questions about English.	← 0—1—2—3—4—5—6—7—8—9—10 →
7. I am an inquisitive teacher and wonder if there are even better ways to teach ELLs.	← 0—1—2—3—4—5—6—7—8—9—10 →
8. More than half of my classes have ELLs in them.	← 0—1—2—3—4—5—6—7—8—9—10 →

Exercise 1.13: Grammar in Multiple Choice Items (HB pp. 1–30)

Read each question and the four answer choices. Circle the correct answer and then decide which of the following grammar points is being tested:

articles
possessive adjectives
verb tenses; active vs. passive voice
verb tenses; modals
verb tenses; verb forms

Multiple Choice Item	Grammar Point Being Tested
1. Veronica _____ at the Sorbonne, but she decided to go to Oxford. (A) studied (B) could have studied (C) had to have studied (D) must have studied	
2. The Statue of Liberty _____ by millions of people every year. (A) visits (B) visited (C) is visits (D) is visited	
3. The horse hurt _____ leg when it tried to jump over the puddle. (A) their (B) its (C) your (D) our	
4. The doctor _____ to check on his patient right now. (A) comes (B) coming (C) is comeing (D) is coming	
5. _____ are very slow animals. (A) A turtles (B) Turtles (C) The turtles (D) An turtles	

Exercise 1.14: Grammar on High-Stakes Tests: Two Formats (HB pp. 1–30)

When grammar is tested in an objective question, the question often appears in one of two ways: as a traditional multiple choice item or as an error identification item. Compare the three examples of these two types of questions.

Multiple Choice Item	Error Identification Item
1a. Barry depended _____ an employment agency to explore all his options. (A) in (C) on (B) for (D) with	1b. The method of <u>house</u> construction <u>in a</u> given area depends mainly <u>to</u> what kinds of materials <u>are</u> readily available.
2a. Melissa spoke _____ to her young son and tried to calm him down. (A) quiet (C) quietly (B) quietish (D) quietful	2b. <u>An</u> itch is a natural signal <u>that</u> our body is <u>quiet</u> responding to <u>the</u> environment.
3a. _____ to classical music is very relaxing. (A) Listen (C) Listens (B) Listening (D) To listening	3b. <u>Listen</u> to segments of a <u>professor's</u> lecture again helps students <u>comprehend</u> the content of the lecture to a much <u>greater</u> degree.

4. Match the grammar point with the correct pair of test questions.

_____ 1a and 1b: A. adjectives and adverbs

_____ 2a and 2b: B. prepositions

_____ 3a and 3b: C. infinitives and gerunds

5. Which of these two question formats do you think is better from the tester's point of view? Why?

_____

_____

_____

_____

6. Which format do you think ELLs find more difficult? Why? Interview ELLs to verify your answers.

_____

_____

_____

_____

Exercise 1.15: Class Observation: Questioning and Wait Time (HB p. 29)

Interactive classes often feature a great deal of questions by the teacher. With ELLs in particular, it is important for teachers to allow sufficient **wait time** between the moment when the teacher poses a question and when the teacher answers the question(s). Observe a class of a teacher that you do not know very well. The class should be an ELL class if possible, but any class will suffice. Do not tell the teacher what exactly you are observing. During the observation, you should:

1. List every question that the teacher asks.
2. Record how many seconds elapse between the question and the answer.
3. Note who gives the answer (e.g., a student, the whole class, or the teacher).

Summarize your findings here in two to five sentences:

_____

_____

_____

_____

_____

_____

_____

_____

_____

Exercise 1.16: Presentation on Generation 1.5 ELLs: Who Are They? (HB p. 30)

Generation 1.5 students are one of the fastest growing groups of learners in the United States and Canada. Gen 1.5ers are often defined as immigrant students who move to the United States at the age of 12 or older and complete their middle school or high school in the United States. The label reflects the group's special place as first-generation Americans who, having migrated to this country during childhood, feel strong identification with the United States but who are native to another country.

Gen 1.5ers graduate with a high school diploma and generally have few problems actually being accepted into college. However, these students have language difficulties in credit courses and present colleges with the quandary of whether these students should be placed in regular courses, ESL or English for Academic Purposes (EAP) courses, or developmental courses. In some areas of the United States, many Generation 1.5 students finish high school with a "certificate of attendance" and not an actual high school diploma. Because of the perceived stigma of ESL courses, many Gen 1.5ers generally prefer to go into developmental composition and developmental reading classes rather than academic ESL. Armed with a high school diploma earned from a curriculum in English, they are offended when they are told they need to "study English" as if they were an international ESL student who has not finished high school in an English-speaking country.

Presentation Project: Working alone or in small groups (as determined by your instructor), search the Internet for at least three sources on Generation 1.5ers. Prepare a short PowerPoint presentation (five to eight slides) on what you have learned. Who are these students? Where are they from? What are their numbers? What are their needs? How are these needs being met? How should their needs be met?

Write the titles of your PowerPoint slides here:

1. _____

2. _____

3. _____

4. _____

5. _____

6. _____

7. _____

8. _____

Exercise 1.17: Generation 1.5 ELLs: A Unique Set of Language Errors (HB p. 30)

Generation 1.5ers may at first appear fluent in conversation but much less so when their grammar is analyzed. While Generation 1.5ers' grammatical errors overlap with those made by ELL students to some degree, there are notable differences. One reason for these differences is that Generation 1.5ers are said to be *ear learners* while ESL students are *eye learners* [Reid, J. (1998). "Eye" and "ear" learners: Identifying the language needs of international students and U.S. resident writers. In P. Byrd & J. Reid (Eds.), *Grammar in the composition classroom*, pp. 3–17. Boston: Heinle & Heinle].

Ear learners (Generation 1.5ers) were immersed in an English-speaking environment and have picked up their English primarily through interaction with native and non-native speakers. In contrast, eye learners (ESLers) have studied and learned English through books and classroom instruction.

Geneneration 1.5ers learned English through listening instead of explicit instruction through grammar, vocabulary, and sentence construction. They know the current "cool" terms used in conversation with their peers, but they cannot follow an academic lecture or textbook prose. Thus, it should come as no surprise that our Gen 1.5ers have strong Basic Interpersonal Communication Skills (BICS, or social language), but they may not have developed the Cognitive Academic Language Proficiency (CALP, or academic language) required for success in college. Epitomizing ear learning, their writing samples are often filled with errors that reflect lack of awareness of grammatical nuances such as word endings that indicate verb tenses, plurals, possessives, or subject-verb agreement. One teacher noted these issues:

> Because many of my Gen 1.5ers have learned English by ear, I often see significant errors in spelling. Several words may be spelled wrong within one line. For example, I had a Gen 1.5 student last semester who spelled "girl" as "gearl." In addition, students may hear a chunk of words and not know they are actually separate words. Many of these students tell me they know they have difficulty with spelling, but they had the impression it wasn't really noticed by people.
>
> Spelling in turn affects their reading ability. While they are doing sustained reading in class, students will ask me what a word means, and once I say the word, they'll say, "Oh, I know what that word means!" They often can't write down correctly what they hear even though they understand what was said. This inability has caused some students to get to the end of their program in health science and then be told they can't do clinicals or even work in a medical office because they can't write things down correctly.

(Personal correspondence, Theresa Pruett-Said, May 20, 2008)

Now read the excerpt on page 16 from an essay written by a Generation 1.5 student who is a freshman in high school. This student was born in the United States. His parents are migrant workers and do not speak English at home. The assignment was to write about a friend. Circle the errors and explain how these errors represent an ear learner.

My Friend

The most funnies thing that Ryan has done is when he was wakebording and one guy that was wakebording to fall out of his wakeboard and Ryan was coming bihind him and Ryan jumped over his head and the guy got scared and screamed wach out and Ryan just laugh.

The things that Ryan likes is to wakeboard and Ride Quads.

Ryan was named after a Irish dancer, Ryan was born in Woodland. He is 14 years old.

Ryan has moved a lot he lived in Chico, Waveland, Summerville, Ocala, Woodland and Richland, Ryan is living in Waveland right know.

Ryan likes to wakeboard hes ben wakebording since he was 12 years old. Ryan also likes to ride quads and he rases all over the place and hes been riding quads sice he was 5 years old and he rides a Honda 450 and hes won a lot of 1st place trophis.

Ryan wants to go to UMC college thas located in Chico. Ryan wants to be a criminal justce police.

Ryan wants to work like a coast guard when he grows.

The other thing that Ryan wants to be is a pro racer for quads or dirtbikes, the most worst thing that had happen to him is that he broke his helment in half in a accident he had when he was racing he only had a few brewses and thats it but he still races until this day.

Ryan's favorite people is Eric Murphay and James Stuward. Eric Murphay is a profecional wake border and James stuwars is a profecional dirtbiker.

2

Basic English Grammar: Usage and Terminology

PRACTICE FOR SECTION 1:
Common Grammar Errors Made by Native Speakers

Exercise 2.01: Identifying Errors with Unnecessary Prepositions (HB pp. 39, 314–315)

Check Yes if the underlined preposition is necessary and correct or No if the underlined preposition is not necessary and should be omitted. Seven of the ten are correct.

	Yes	No
1. John wanted to know what was going <u>on</u>.		
2. James is a person everyone can depend <u>on</u>.		
3. If you are looking for a restaurant in a city that you do not know well, it is difficult to know where to go <u>to</u>.		
4. Where have you been buying your produce <u>at</u>?		
5. Which mall did you buy those shoes <u>at</u>?		
6. That is the actor Ashley is crazy <u>about</u>.		
7. This is his favorite band to listen <u>to</u>.		
8. Tonight is the concert I have been waiting <u>for</u>.		
9. Where is your family living <u>at</u>?		
10. Who is that person your sister is talking <u>to</u>?		

Exercise 2.02: Identifying and Editing Errors with *I* and *me* (HB pp. 39, 315–316)

Identify and correct any grammatical errors in these sentences. Three of the ten are correct.

1. Between you and I, it seems that I don't think I can trust him anymore.

2. James, Laura, and me have been invited to a birthday party on Sunday.

3. My sister and I have been fortunate to see our grandparents live into their nineties.

4. When our boss came back from Italy, he decided to create a new international division that included Tim, Rodrigo, and I.

5. It has been difficult for my husband and I to take time off at the same time.

6. I have always wanted to visit Japan. My friend and I finally got a chance to go last summer.

7. The best thing that could happen as a result of our recent problems is for my brother and I to keep in touch more often.

8. My sister and me have always found foreign languages fascinating.

9. The tickets to the show were given to Brenda and me, so there are no more tickets for anyone else.

10. People like Ed and I do the best work because we are naturally very organized.

Exercise 2.03: Identifying and Editing Errors with *myself* (HB pp. 39, 317)

Identify and correct any grammatical errors in these sentences. Three of the ten are correct.

1. It was going to be a long drive from Florida to Rhode Island, so John and myself decided to stop for rest breaks every six hours.

2. Since I was a child, when something needed to be done right, my mother always told me to do it myself rather than asking for someone's help.

3. Most people in my office take their vacations in July or August. As for myself, September is the best month to take my vacation because flights are cheaper then.

4. The tickets to the football game on Saturday afternoon are for Kelly and myself, so the rest of you will have to buy your own tickets as soon as possible.

5. Some people might find it surprising, but both Ian and myself enjoy long flights because we finally get to see new movie releases we always miss due to our busy schedules.

6. When I cook, I like to prepare the entire meal from beginning to end all by myself as this is the only way to control the ingredients and the amount of spice that goes in.

7. Driving is not something I enjoy doing very much, but it is absolutely necessary to make myself feel independent.

8. I wish I knew what the future holds for myself.

9. The love of gardening is something that I inherited from my father, who used to spend hours with myself digging in the garden.

10. I have always wanted to visit Korea, but I don't think that I would truly enjoy the experience were I to travel by myself because I'd have to leave my husband home.

Exercise 2.04: Identifying and Editing Errors with Past Participles and Past Tense (HB pp. 39, 318)

Identify and edit any errors in past participle usage. Three of the ten are correct.

1. The factory could have took more than five years to build, but the workers managed to finish the construction project in slightly more than three years.

2. It is too late to do the laundry now. I really should have did it earlier.

3. I could have drank the whole bottle of water, but I didn't.

4. Since I moved here to New York, I've seen so many great Broadway shows.

5. If the tickets were cheaper, all of the girls would have went to the concert.

6. Having looked at dozens of designs for weeks, Marie has finally chosen her wedding dress.

7. What a horrible accident! The driver of the blue car said she seen something dart out in front of her vehicle, so she swerved to avoid hitting it.

8. Rita will have to buy a new watch since her old one is broke.

9. Being broke is something that happens to all of us at some time.

10. Had he knew that his friend was sick, he would have taken him some medicine.

Exercise 2.05: Distinguishing Usage of *lie* and *lay* (HB pp. 39, 319)

Underline the correct form of the verb in each sentence.

1. Maria's grandfather (lie, lay, laid) the foundation of the family business 40 years ago.

2. Only a few people can (lay, lie) down and take a power nap almost anywhere.

3. Dermatologists warn people to avoid (laying, lying) out in the sun so much.

4. When was the last time you (lie, lied, lay, laid) down on the grass and looked up into the blue sky?

5. The construction company has been (laying, lying) the bricks with record speeds in order to finish the building as scheduled.

6. The contracts (laying, lying) on the desk have not been signed yet.

7. Have you ever (lay, laid, lain, lied) on a water bed before? It is said to relieve back pain.

8. We found a turtle (laying, lying) on its back.

9. When Joe finally told the truth and (lay, laid, lied, lain) the proverbial cards on the table, we all felt guilty for not seeing what he was going through.

10. It is time to get up and do something productive. You have (lay, lied, lain, laid) in bed watching TV half the day.

Exercise 2.06: Identifying and Editing Errors with *whoever* and *whomever (who* and *whom)* (HB pp. 39, 320)

Correct any errors in the use of *whoever, whomever, who,* or *whom.* **Three of the ten are correct.**

1. Whomever told you about the trip did not provide you with all the necessary details.

2. When I want to go see a movie, I ask my friend Rosa, whom knows all about the latest releases, which one I should see.

3. One of my best friends, whom I have known since first grade, decided to move to China to teach English.

4. Please meet Mario, my good friend from Portugal and one of our international friends who my husband and I took a trip with to Barcelona last summer.

5. Every Monday night when I am flipping through channels looking for something interesting, I find the show with the guy who travels to exotic places and eats bizarre foods.

6. The committee members differed as to who they should choose as the chairperson.

7. It is difficult to find the persons whom are responsible for that car accident as a few cars left the scene right away.

8. Please give these shoes to whomever wants to have them. They are not my size.

9. No matter what my sister does, she is one person who I cannot be mad at for a long time.

10. Please look over the various candidates' portfolios and then select whoever most clearly has the best set of materials.

Exercise 2.07: Identifying and Editing Errors with *he/she/it don't* (HB pp. 39, 321–322)

Identify and correct grammatical errors with *he/she/it don't* in these sentences. Three of the ten have no errors.

1. No one can understand why the president of those companies don't hire more workers from our local area.

2. No matter how many times I tell her how to fold the napkins, she still don't do it the right way.

3. Of course we wish you all the best in your new job. However, if your new job don't work out well, you know you are always welcome to come back here to this position.

4. Even when there is a crisis all around us, sometimes we humans don't understand how difficult the situation really is.

5. A lot of people believe that it don't matter if you vote because they see politics as some kind of game.

6. They have to change planes in Denver, but they don't have to rush. Their flight arrives in Denver at noon, and then their next flight doesn't leave until 3:30.

7. According to this email, everyone has to change account passwords today. You can do this now, or you can wait until just before we close. I've read the email several times, and the message don't say exactly when we have to do this.

8. The boss asked me to check this flyer, and I don't see any errors in it. In fact, Joseph and Susan looked at it as well and concur. We've gone through the information several times, and the content and layout don't appear to have any mistakes of any type.

9. When people start exercise programs, they have to be disciplined and focused. It just don't make any sense to pay for a gym membership if they are not serious about using it.

10. The position that we are trying to fill requires experience in supervising others. After perusing your resume, I don't see that you have this experience. To get this job, you need this experience in this area. For our business purposes, it don't matter how long you supervised others, but you definitely need to have that kind of experience.

Exercise 2.08: Identifying and Editing Errors with *if I would have known* (HB pp. 39, 323)

Identify and correct any grammatical errors in these items. Three of the ten are correct.

1. Joe was unable to make his mortgage payment this month. His sister would have been more understanding and lent him the money if Joe would not have just spent a month in Paris.

2. My friend's grandfather passed away last night. If I would have known that she couldn't afford the airfare to go home to attend the funeral, I would have been the first person to help her out.

3. I was offered a job in Germany last year. If I would have accepted it, you would have been able to stay with me for free when you visited Germany last month.

4. If I had known that you were trying to get in touch with me for hours last night, I would have put my cell phone on vibrate instead of turning it off.

5. They would not have met and then gotten married three years later if they would not have attended the same university.

6. Even small noises annoy me. If I had known that the new video card for my computer would be making so much noise, I would not have bought it in the first place.

7. It would have been impossible for Jane to get her new job if the committee members would not have known how hard-working and dedicated she was.

8. If Andres would not have brought all that carry-on luggage with him, he would have cleared the security check point much faster.

9. Julio would have missed his flight if he had not asked his friend to give him a ride to the airport.

10. Every time tires are changed, they are supposed to be rotated, balanced, and aligned. If my husband would have had his new tires balanced, he would not have been bothered by all the noise they were making.

Exercise 2.09: Identifying and Editing Errors with Double Negatives (HB pp. 39, 324–325)

Identify and correct any errors with double negatives in these items. Three of the ten are correct.

1. I have no idea how Daniela graduated from college. She hardly ever opened a book.

2. You should have asked me to help you earlier. I don't have no problem doing it when I can plan accordingly.

3. We need to go grocery shopping. The refrigerator does not have no food in it. What are we supposed to eat for dinner tonight?

4. I thought I kept all of the receipts for big purchases, but since we moved into our new house, I can't seem to find none of them.

5. You are the first person that ever asked me this question. No one has never done that before.

6. I don't like either tea or coffee. I prefer sparkling mineral water, which is hard to find in some restaurants, so I often have to settle for club soda.

7. I am a big fan of the performing arts. Seldom do I miss an opportunity to see a play, a Broadway musical, or a ballet.

8. After tornadoes hit North Carolina last month, none of the police or the firefighters had no time to rest.

9. Marshall is stubborn. He is the kind of person who does not agree with nothing anyone else says. He thinks he is always right.

10. Please leave! Do not call, text, or email me no more. I don't want to see or hear from you. I want you out of my life.

Exercise 2.10: Identifying and Editing Errors with *bad* and *badly* (HB pp. 39, 325)

In these items, identify and correct grammatical errors with the distinction between *bad* and *badly*. Three of the ten are correct.

1. My friend got into a car accident yesterday night. He seems to be injured so bad that he will have to spend at least a month in the hospital.

2. Last night their children behaved badly, and today Mr. and Mrs. Thompson are trying to figure out what to do. In the meantime, the Thompsons have agreed not to take their children to eat in a restaurant until all of them can sit quietly at the table for more than five minutes.

3. Without a doubt, his Spanish is deficient. His grammar is full of errors, and he writes badly. His grade of F reflects his poor results in this course.

4. Laura wanted to win the race bad, so for more than a year, she ran five miles every day before she went to work.

5. Connie overslept and felt so badly about not arriving at her appointment on time.

6. I heard about your accident. Are you all right? How bad was your car damaged?

7. I can't stand the smell of cheese. In particular, limburger cheese smells really bad.

8. When the bride tripped on her long dress and fell down right there in the church, everyone felt so badly for her, but what could we do?

9. What is in this soup? I can't eat it. It just tastes badly.

10. People who live in glass houses should not throw stones. To me, this saying means that we should not speak bad about another person.

Exercise 2.11: Identifying and Editing Errors with *them* and *those* (HB pp. 39, 326)

Identify and correct grammatical errors in these items. Three of the ten are correct.

1. As soon as you have filled out those forms that I gave you this morning, could you please help me send them to the appropriate department heads?

2. I like what you said in your eulogy. Most of us who heard you agree that them words that you used were especially important to the family.

3. In this slide, we can see some lenticular clouds. Lenticular clouds, which look like a stack of pancakes, always form near mountains. Look at the clouds above this mountain on the right. As you can see, them clouds are elliptical but with points on both sides. An interesting point about those clouds is that they don't move. Instead of moving with the wind like normal clouds, lenticular clouds are stationary. The wind blows right through them.

4. Some families have certain health needs that involve rare diseases for which there is no inexpensive treatment. The new health initiative will certainly reach them families that have those health needs.

5. I know that the sign says that they're on sale, but I don't think those pants that you have in your hand are really a good buy.

6. If you'd like your caladiums to have colorful foliage again next year, you must take care of the bulbs. You'll need to dig them bulbs up this fall and carefully store them. That's also the case for canna lilies, tulips, and gladiolas.

7. Do you really want to buy those shoes? They don't look very good on you, so I'd recommend trying them other shoes with the blue strap.

8. Have you tried Martha's biscuits? Everyone says that they would pay good money for them biscuits if they were available at a restaurant.

9. The election results from yesterday were split. Voters in Indiana favored the Democrat, but voters in West Virginia favored the Republican. Newspapers wrote extensively today about them results, but many people are just tired of hearing this news.

10. Our boss told us that the memos from our headquarters don't indicate a problem with our company. Many of us telephone operators have read them and don't concur. The tone in those memos is unmistakably negative and almost caustic.

Exercise 2.12: Identifying and Editing Errors with *have* and *of* (HB pp. 39, 326–327)

Identify and correct grammatical errors in these items. Three of the ten are correct.

1. One of my biggest regrets is that I never graduated from high school. All my life, I have had to take jobs with less pay as a result. In hindsight, I really should of stayed in school.

2. There are many places where we could have gone for our vacation, but after weeks of checking out sites on the Internet, we chose Denver, Colorado.

3. Who might of done this? This kind of crime just makes no sense.

4. If I had known of your award, I certainly would of called immediately to congratulate you.

5. Look at these blood stains. The killer must of attacked him here and then dragged the body over there. At least, that's what this blood trail would seem to indicate.

6. What could the kidnapper's motive be? I can't think of any reason why someone might of done this to that family. What about you? What are your thoughts?

7. I can't imagine how bad you felt when you didn't get that job. You must of been devastated. If there is anything that I can do to help, please let me know.

8. It is important to practice tennis every day if you want to improve your game. If I had learned to play the game earlier and had had a daily practice regimen, who knows how far I could have gone in the sport?

9. Your password is too easy to figure out, so it's no wonder that someone got into your account. The number of letters and the pattern of the numbers in your password should make unauthorized access of your account difficult. You really should have come up with a better password.

10. If I had been the manager there, I would have done things really differently. My opinion is that the manager should of fired those employees on the spot. They were guilty of bad work and perhaps bad judgment.

Exercise 2.13: Distinguishing Usage of *it's*, *its*, and *its'* (HB pp. 39, 327–328)

Underline the correct form of *it's*, *its*, and *its'* in the sentences in this paragraph about a common household item. As you read, can you guess what the item is?

①(It's, Its, Its') something that everyone has at home. ②(It's, Its, Its') shapes, colors, and sizes may vary, and ③(it's, its, its') mostly made out of plastic. Some people choose to hide ④(it's, its, its') wires and cords, but that's not necessary at all. It may have ⑤(it's, its, its') own stand, or ⑥(it's, its, its') possible to hang it on the wall. ⑦(It's, Its, Its') prices keep going down all the time, which is a general trend these days with anything that has a plug. ⑧(It's, Its, Its') in every house, but ⑨(it's, its, its') exact location within the houses varies. In fact, you might have this item in your kitchen, living room, or bedroom. ⑩(It's, Its, Its') a very useful thing to have if you want to watch some news or your favorite shows. Do you know what this object is?

Exercise 2.14: Identifying Errors with *your* and *you're* (HB pp. 39, 329)

Identify and correct seven grammatical errors with *your* and *you're* usage in this text.

Have you ever been to Venice? I think that you're spirits will be lifted by visiting Venice. Most tourists arrive in Venice by train. As you step out of the railway station, right away your facing the Canal Grande, its main water artery. After wandering the small *campi* (parts) of Venice, crossing bridge after bridge, you will soon find yourself at another magnificent spectacle, Saint Mark's Square, where your made aware of how small and insignificant your feeling at this moment in comparison to the ageless beauty of the square and its central masterpiece, Saint Mark's Cathedral.

Your impression of Venice changes after dark. With waves of tourists gone, piazzas are breathing again, gondolas slowly moving on the water, and on Saint Mark's Square, the bands start their nightly competition for you're attention, playing music from all over the world.

Don't try to see Venice in one day. Allow it to reveal itself. You'll be surprised and rewarded with side trips to the islands of Murano and Burano, which are world famous for their glass-blowing factories and lace, respectively. When it comes to a visit to Venice, your age does not matter because there is something here for people of all ages. It does not matter how many times you have visited *la serenissima repubblica di Venezia* (the Most Serene Republic of Venice, as it was once called). It always seems to call you back and soon your waiting for that next trip as if it were you're first. You're certainly in for a real treat in this great city.

Exercise 2.15: Errors with 's (HB pp. 39, 330)

Correct the four errors with 's in this joke.

One day a driver was taking a truckload of penguin's from the airport to the zoo. The penguins had just arrived in the city from the North Pole. On the way to the zoo, the truck's radiator overheated, and the driver was trying to figure out how to get the penguins to their destination as quickly as possible. The truck drivers' requests for a repair truck were getting no reply, so he was in a bit of a panic.

He flagged down a van that was passing by. The truck driver pleaded with the van driver for help. "Here's $100 to take these penguins to the zoo. Can you do this?"

The van driver's response was an immediate "Yes, certainly." Through the driver's amazing teamwork, they transferred the penguins to the van in a matter of minutes, and then the van driver started driving toward the zoo.

A repair truck finally showed up and took care of the truck's mechanical problem. After his truck was fixed, the truck driver drove as fast as he could to the zoo to make sure the penguins were all right. As he got near the zoo, he was shocked to see the van full of penguins driving away from the zoo. The truck driver turned around his truck and drove as fast as he could to catch up with the van. He flashed his lights and honked his horn to get the van driver to pull over to the side of the road.

The truck driver got out of his truck and walked over to the van. "What are you doing? I gave you $100 to take the penguins to the zoo!" The van drivers calm response explained it all: "I did take them to the zoo, but we had about $35 left over, so I thought I'd take them to the park now."

Exercise 2.16: Identifying and Editing Errors with *who's* and *whose* (HB pp. 39, 331)

Identify and correct grammatical errors in these items. Three of the ten are correct.

1. When I started working at Brown & Sons, it took me a while to figure out whose in charge since I was receiving orders from three people.

2. The graduate admissions office at any university is primarily looking for people who's GRE score is over 1,000 for two out of three sections of the test.

3. My neighbor Colin, whose car was stolen last night, filed a police report, and they promised to find who is responsible for the theft.

4. My friend whose mother has been battling cancer has been doing everything possible to make her comfortable after her chemo treatments.

5. In the United States, a person whose had a glass of wine can still get behind the wheel and drive. In some countries, that's unacceptable.

6. Recently I met a woman who's life was full of unpleasant surprises. She would say that she attracts bad luck.

7. The president whose in charge in 2020 will certainly have a daunting task in leading our country at that time.

8. When a person is unhappy, his or her problems are unique. However, each person whose happy is happy all the same. With this idea, Leo Tolstoy started his famous work *Anna Karenina.*

9. Last week I attended a reception in Dr. White's honor. I am lucky to know a person whose been awarded a Pulitzer Prize.

10. Whose car should we take? Brian's is bigger as it is an SUV. We might be more comfortable in it considering the long trip ahead.

Exercise 2.17: Distinguishing Usage of *to, too,* and *two* (HB pp. 39, 332)

Underline the correct forms to complete this passage about buying a new house.

When looking for a new house, the most important thing ① (to, too, two) do is to consider this purchase very carefully. It is important ② (to, too, two) do some research ③ (to, too, two) find out the prices in the neighborhood you are interested in as you don't want ④ (to, too, two) pay ⑤ (to, too, two) much for that house.

It is not a bad idea ⑥ (to, too, two) limit your search ⑦ (to, too, two) ⑧ (to, too, two) or three houses on the same street and visit them ⑨ (to, too, two) see which one you like best. Meeting the neighbors when possible is a good idea, ⑩ (to, too, two), since you might end up living next ⑪ (to, too, two) someone who likes ⑫ (to, too, two) throw loud parties all night long. Another thing you should consider is whether there is a homeowners' association and how much you would need ⑬ (to, too, two) pay per month. In some communities, the fees are ⑭ (to, too, two) high and even if you have a good mortgage payment, having ⑮ (to, too, two) house mortgages per month would be problematic. Many other things should be considered before a decision is made ⑯ (to, too, two) buy a house, but these are the most basic considerations.

Exercise 2.18: Identifying and Editing Errors with *affect* and *effect* (HB pp. 39, 333)

Identify and correct grammatical errors in these items. Three of the ten are correct.

1. The loss of her father has effected her behavior. She has become moody and irritable.

2. These days some people are concerned about green house gasses, global warming, and their affects on our planet.

3. Some people consider the original three "Star Wars" movies classics and better than the more recently filmed ones. Others prefer the newer trilogy for its special effects, elaborate costumes, and creative visuals.

4. Amendment 10 was supported by the electorate as well as the State Senate and will go into affect next month.

5. It was hard to tell if she was truly sorry for what she had done or if her tears were simply for effect. No one ever knew her to be overly emotional.

6. Because Brian did not pay last month's rent, his credit was effected.

7. She was greatly affected by the letter she received from her friend from whom she had not heard in years.

8. The board agreed to what was in affect a reduction in medical benefits to all company employees.

9. Studying day and night had its affects. Jose was able to pass the TOEFL® the first time he took it.

10. His father's words deeply effected him, and he decided from that point on that he would never again do anything that could disappoint his dad.

Exercise 2.19: Identifying and Editing Errors with *lose* and *loose* (HB pp. 39, 334)

Identify and correct grammatical errors in these items. Three of the ten are correct.

1. On Friday after Thanksgiving, a lot of people wake up early to go bargain hunting. It is very easy to loose one's head and buy things that are not needed with such low prices.

2. John's mom was getting ready to play the role of the tooth fairy again as one of John's teeth had been loose for days.

3. There is hardly any other area that has such job security as the academic world. Once a professor has been awarded tenure, it is virtually impossible to loose that job.

4. Ann was surprised to find a lose alligator in her pool when she came home from work last night.

5. It is unnatural for a parent to lose a child, but it happens. For example, more than 6,000 teenagers in the United States die every year in car accidents.

6. I am very careful when talking about politics to my brother. He is a lose cannon and has a hard time controlling his anger when politics is being discussed.

7. If our party's candidates do not start agreeing on the topics that matter and show unity, we are likely to loose votes in the upcoming election.

8. Impressionists have been admired all over the world for the unique lose brushwork and humanism of their paintings.

9. The gymnast is training hard. She knows that she cannot afford to lose her balance on the beam during the competition.

10. Hollywood is leading the world's obsession with dieting to loose weight.

Exercise 2.20: Identifying Errors with *they're, there,* and *their* (HB pp. 39, 335)

Identify and correct the seven errors with *they're, there,* and *their* in this text about college life.

Arguably, college years are the best in anyone's life. In some countries, students live care-free lives, partying as much as they can, and all their expected to do is attend classes and do well. There are countries in the world where students do not have part-time jobs or rent to pay. They live with there parents until they graduate or even until they get married. They're parents pay for there education even if the family is not very well off. In the United States, things are a bit different. Sometimes students not only go to school full-time but also manage to juggle a couple of part-time jobs. It is obvious that the quality of their college work might suffer from such tight schedules, but there paying rent and other bills and are therefore forced to prioritize. Wouldn't it be great if students getting a college education did not need to worry about there bills, loans, and other financial responsibilities? So many young minds and hours would be freed and could be used to benefit the world. This may be a bit idealistic, but their is always hope.

Exercise 2.21: Review: Identifying and Editing Grammar Errors Made by Native Speakers (HB pp. 39, 313–335)

Identify and correct grammar errors in these items. Each item has two or three errors.

1. Joe and Sue would not have helped if they would have known the real cause of my money problem's.

2. When I lived in Brazil, Andrea and me often went shopping together because I hated doing it by myself. However, we never lay our bags in plain sight in the car because it was not safe.

3. Even though Andres has been criticized by his boss countless times, he don't pay attention to his comments. In fact, they don't make him feel badly at all.

4. Its common knowledge these days that a passenger can carry only one or too small items on the plane.

5. My friend had never drank ice wine until his trip to Canada. After trying it, he said that it did not taste badly. He found it to be very sweet.

6. My grandmother don't care who comes for dinner. Anyone whose hungry is always welcome.

7. It is widely known that second-hand smoke effects non-smokers even though their not exposed to nicotine directly.

8. Jane was about to loose her cool. She should of been at the airport an hour ago. In all likelihood, she was going to miss her flight.

9. Where are we meeting at? I will catch up with you guys in a minute. I need to check that no one picked up none of the packages I left by the door.

10. I should have drove that car a bit more before I bought it. Its making funny noises now.

Exercise 2.22: Review: Identifying and Editing Grammar Errors Made by Native Speakers (HB pp. 39, 313–335)

Identify and correct 17 grammar errors made by native speakers in this text.

Let's review. By now, you should of been made aware of 20 native speaker mistakes. Some of these errors are more common and unfortunately occur to often in writing and speaking. As a teacher, your a prime example for your ELLs, so your use of correct grammar should extend far beyond this book. Imagine if you had a teacher whom made grammar mistakes. Would you loose respect for that instructor? Wouldn't you feel badly? Its hard to imagine such a thing until you put yourself in your students shoes. As a teacher, you are the person whose responsible for the accuracy of the information their getting. That you are not very sure about the rules yet don't matter. Practice and experience will help. Teachers' have a profound affect on each students' learning. Its up to you to do the best job possible to help them learners. If not you, then whom?

PRACTICE FOR SECTION 2:
Eight Parts of Speech

Exercise 2.23: Identifying Nouns (HB pp. 44–46)

Early literacy often includes children's riddles. Find and underline the 15 nouns in these children's riddles about cats and dogs. (Do not count the word *riddle.*)

Riddle 1. There are ten baby cats in a big box and one cat jumps out. How many kittens are left? None. They are all copycats!

Riddle 2. Why did the dog continue to run in circles? He was a watchdog and needed winding.

Riddle 3. How do you know when your cat has been using your computer? When your mouse has cat teeth marks on it.

Riddle 4. Where should you never take a dog? A flea market.

Exercise 2.24: Uses of –s Endings (HB pp. 44–47)

Each of the 30 underlined words in this passage ends in –s. This ending often indicates a plural noun, but this ending has three different usages, including plural of nouns *(cats)*, third person singular *(he/she/it)* of verbs *(requires)*, and possessive of nouns *(Emily's).* Write PL above plural nouns, V above the singular verbs, and POSS above the possessive forms.

In her book *Learning Style* ① *Perspectives*: *Impact in the Classroom*, Lynne Sarasin ② advises ③ teachers to keep current with ④ methodologies and ⑤ strategies on learning ⑥ styles to be able to change teaching ⑦ strategies and ⑧ techniques to maximize the learning potential of each student. She ⑨ points out the importance of accommodating diverse learning ⑩ styles in a fair and positive classroom environment. ⑪ Sarasin's book ⑫ enumerates seven multiple ⑬ intelligences introduced by Gardner. She ⑭ notes that primary sense learning style classification (visual, auditory, tactile or kinesthetic) is easy to incorporate into lesson ⑮ plans. She then ⑯ addresses four ⑰ steps to more effective teaching. She also ⑱ provides a preliminary diagnostic tool (debriefing) to identify learning ⑲ styles. She ⑳ admits that a given ㉑ teacher's class usually ㉒ reflects a combination of that ㉓ teacher's learning style and the way in which he or she was taught more successfully. The author of these ㉔ ideas ㉕ concludes by stating that all ㉖ students should know which learning ㉗ styles they use in order to benefit from their ㉘ strengths, which then ㉙ results in student motivation and increased academic achievement. This ㉚ author's work is a great contribution to education.

Source: Sarasin, L.C. (1998). *Learning style perspectives: Impact in the classroom.* Madison, WI: Atwood.

Exercise 2.25: Identifying and Editing ELL Errors with Nouns (HB pp. 44–46)

Underline the ELL mistake with noun usage in these items. Then identify the type of error, and write a correction above it.

1. omission of plural *–s*	5. no article with count nouns
2. unnecessary plural *–s*	6. *the* with abstract nouns
3. wrong noun ending	7. not capitalizing proper nouns
4. plural non-count nouns	

1. _____ Some people believe that criminals need help to recuperate from different mental ills.

2. _____ I need to go to my friend's house on maple street.

3. _____ Juan went to the store to buy loaf of bread.

4. _____ However, if it is over level four, several problem happen.

5. _____ It is the same process for children in every countries.

6. _____ I don't like when the teacher gives us a lot of homeworks.

7. _____ Some people believe the life is the result of hard work, not luck.

8. _____ I like to watch movie every weekend.

9. _____ We have earthquake in Japan. They're fairly common.

10. _____ We bought a lot of new furnitures when we moved to our new house.

11. _____ I went overseas in september and stayed for six months.

12. _____ We really think you should continue your guitar studies. You have the real talent.

13. _____ Today I needed to send fax to my country, but I did not know where to do it.

14. _____ I have been in the U.S. for five month, and I like it here very much.

15. _____ Each students needs to get 550 on the paper-based TOEFL® test.

Exercise 2.26: Identifying Common and Proper Nouns (HB p. 45)

In the following text, underline all common nouns once and proper nouns twice.

Above West Michigan: Aerial Photography of West Michigan **by Marge Beaver**

These stunning bird's eye views offer rare and beautiful glimpses of West Michigan's rivers, lakes, and shoreline from the lofty perch of the camera lens of Marge Beaver. Her breathtaking four-season photographs transform our view of Michigan into a magical land. From the working harbors and lights along Lake Michigan, to the playful inland lakes, to the fruit-covered orchards, spectacular flowers, and fun-filled festivals, these are images of Michigan as you've never seen her before. All of these, plus arresting photographs of winding highways, snake-like rivers, and city harbors make this book a collector's item for anyone who loves this beautiful state.

Published by the *University of Michigan Press.*

Exercise 2.27: Identifying Concrete and Abstract Nouns (HB p. 45)

Find and underline all the nouns in these items. Write CONC above the concrete nouns and ABST above the abstract nouns. The number in parentheses indicates the total number of nouns.

1. The trial finally finished. Justice has been served for all the betrayal and deceit that cost taxpayers millions. (6)

2. James was always known for his attention to details. His dedication has earned him respect among colleagues. (6)

3. Patience is a virtue. (2)

4. Maria discovered a perfect way to achieve relaxation and relieve the stress she gets in the office. She practices yoga twice a week. (7)

5. No matter how funny a joke may be, some people may not be able to appreciate it. (2)

6. You need to watch your child because now that she can walk, her natural curiosity may get her in trouble even in the safest places around the house. (5)

7. The fastest way to achieve inner peace is through honesty. (3)

8. Someone once said that talent is 95 percent hard work and 5 percent luck. (3)

9. Helena and her husband celebrated the success of the last album they released where he played the piano and she sang. (5)

10. Her pride comes through in everything she does. It is difficult for anyone to truly believe in her friendship. (2)

Exercise 2.28: Identifying Count Nouns and Non-Count Nouns (HB p. 46)

In the following proverbs, underline all the nouns. Then write C above count nouns and NC above non-count nouns.

1. Every cloud has a silver lining.

2. Charity begins at home.

3. Where there's smoke, there's fire.

4. Money talks.

5. Barking dogs seldom bite.

6. All that glitters is not gold.

7. Don't put all your eggs in one basket.

8. Silence is golden.

Exercise 2.29: Identifying Verbs (Simple Predicates) (HB pp. 46–51)

Underline all the verbs (simple predicates) in the following text. The first one has been done for you.

In this intriguing article, Christinson <u>talks</u> about brain-research application for ESL classroom. She emphasizes the importance of the limbic system and students' emotional self-regulation for teaching. She describes four pathways of recalling information: procedural, episodic, semantic, and sensory. She explains that episodic memory provides important clues concerning the retention of information as people usually remember emotionally hooked events, which can be successfully used in teaching. Semantic memory is of no less importance because it is used for remembering concepts and general knowledge, which does not depend on the context. Then she addresses factors which affect attention such as novelty, need, emotion, and meaning. The author notes that emotion is a key factor in both attention and learning. The brain is a pattern-seeking device, and each student's brain constructs a unique meaning.

Exercise 2.30: Identifying and Editing Errors with Verbs (HB pp. 46–51)

Underline the ELL mistake with verb usage in these sentences. Then identify the type of error, and write a correction above it.

1. misuse of *have* for *be*	6. simple present instead of present perfect
2. lack of 3rd person singular endings	7. switching verb tenses
3. auxiliary/negating	8. no direct object with transitive verb
4. auxiliary/question	9. infinitives after modals
5. simple present instead of present progressive	

1. _____ She cooked a wonderful meal, and the guests enjoy it.

2. _____ Whom you invite to see a movie with us?

3. _____ Today is my birthday. I have twenty years old now.

4. _____ We found a great TV at the mall and bought.

5. _____ Jane like to walk her dog in the park. It make her happy.

6. _____ They might to want to go see that show next week.

7. _____ They want to buy a new house. They look at one now.

8. _____ I no like Jane. She talks all the time.

9. _____ What do you do now? Are you busy?

10. _____ They could to take a train or rent a car to get there.

11. _____ After a long walk, we have very thirsty now. Do you have any water?

12. _____ Juan is not a good student. He not come to class on time.

13. _____ Since visiting Europe, Tom takes a new interest in foreign languages.

14. _____ I visit Disney World three times already.

15. _____ They live in New York for five years.

Exercise 2.31: Distinguishing Transitive and Intransitive Verb Usage (HB p. 48)

In Numbers 1 and 2, write sentences using the verbs *begin* and *move* first as transitive (VT) and then as intransitive (VI). Do the same in Number 3 with a verb of your choice.

1. *begin*

   vt: _____

   _____

   vi: _____

   _____

2. *move*

   vt: _____

   _____

   vi: _____

   _____

3. your verb: _____

   vt: _____

   _____

   vi: _____

   _____

Exercise 2.32: Distinguishing Linking Verbs and Main Verbs (HB p. 48)

Circle the underlined verbs that are linking verbs. One sentence does not have any.

1. Tim's mother <u>is</u> still in the hospital, but her condition <u>remains</u> stable. Doctors <u>are saying</u> that the recovery process <u>may take</u> several months.

2. Having a picnic in the park <u>sounds</u> like a great idea. I'<u>ll make</u> a shopping list, and you <u>should call</u> up friends and <u>invite</u> them to join us.

3. When Linda <u>turned</u> 50, she <u>decided</u> to celebrate by hiking through the woods.

4. Kevin <u>looked</u> upset. We did not <u>know</u> if he <u>got</u> into an argument with his wife, or if things <u>were not going</u> well at work.

5. It <u>seemed</u> strange that Maria did not <u>write</u> anyone for a month after she <u>went</u> back to Chile.

6. My mom's banana bread <u>smells</u> wonderful, but it <u>tastes</u> even better with a tall glass of her refreshing home-made iced tea.

7. It soon <u>became</u> apparent that she would not be able to join us since she <u>was</u> still very sick.

8. My grandfather <u>lived</u> a long life. He <u>fought</u> during WWII, <u>had</u> three sons and 12 grandkids, and <u>lived</u> a long life.

Exercise 2.33: Distinguishing Auxiliary Verbs and Main Verbs (HB pp. 48–51)

Write AUX or V above to indicate whether the underlined forms of the verbs are auxiliary (AUX) or main verbs (V).

1. She <u>has</u> <u>been</u> a good friend of mine since high school. We <u>have</u> <u>done</u> a lot of silly things together over the years.

2. I <u>am</u> planning to visit my aunt who <u>has</u> a house on the Florida coast. When I <u>am</u> there, all we <u>do</u> is rest and catch up on things that <u>have</u> happened since we last saw each other.

3. The students <u>are</u> taking a grammar test. They <u>have</u> 20 more minutes left.

4. Every professor on a 12-month teaching contract <u>has</u> six weeks of paid vacation a year. It <u>is</u> great to be able to take time off. However, Dr. Jenks <u>does</u> not <u>do</u> that.

5. He <u>is</u> dreaming again instead of working. I wish he'd shape up and start taking his job seriously. He needs to do a good job on the project that his boss assigned him.

6. The fridge <u>is</u> almost empty. We'<u>ve</u> <u>been</u> cooking a lot at home this week. Let's <u>do</u> some shopping later tonight.

7. He <u>does</u> not like his new apartment. It <u>is</u> not as spacious as his old one, and it only <u>has</u> one window.

8. They <u>were</u> forced to give up their house after not paying the mortgage for six months. Now they <u>live</u> in the smallest place that they <u>have</u> ever <u>had</u>.

9. I <u>did</u> my best on the test last Monday, but I still <u>did</u> not <u>do</u> as well as my brother <u>did</u>.

10. Joe's life <u>is</u> great. He just got married and moved into a lovely apartment he <u>has</u> in the city.

Exercise 2.34: Identifying *be* and *have* as Auxiliary and Main Verbs (HB pp. 48–50)

Underline all forms of the verbs *be* and *have* in this joke. Then write AUX or V above them to indicate whether they are auxiliary or main verbs.

There was a huge psychiatrists' convention in town for the week. One afternoon, after the psychiatrists had attended numerous sessions, three psychiatrists had had enough of the conference and decided to go out for a walk.

The first one said, "You know, people are always coming to us with all of their problems, but I never have a chance to tell anyone about my issues."

The other two concurred, and one of them said, "Hey, why don't we each tell what is bothering us? We're all professionals, so we have the skills to help each other, right?" They all agreed that this was a great idea.

The first psychiatrist confessed, "I have been hiding something for most of my adult life. I am a compulsive shopper. I am always shopping for things in stores and online. I am completely in debt, and I am forced to charge my patients exorbitant fees so I can make ends meet."

The second psychiatrist began, "I have had a drug problem for years. In fact, it's completely out of control, and it's ruining my life. I don't know how much longer I can bear to keep it a secret."

The third said, "I know that it's wrong, but no matter how hard I try, I just cannot keep a secret."

Exercise 2.35: Identifying Modal Verbs (HB p. 51)

Find and underline 12 modal verbs in this paragraph about buying a car.

When you are thinking about purchasing a car, a few things should be considered. First of all, you need to know how far you would drive the car and how big it ought to be. If you are a family of four or more, a mini-van might be an option, but having that kind of a vehicle will not leave much money in your wallet with current gas prices. Some people might favor foreign cars and consider some Japanese models to be among the most reliable, economical, and long-lasting ones. You may want to visit a few dealerships before you make a final decision. In addition, smart shoppers should do research online these days and walk into the dealership with a clear picture of what is needed in order to save time and money. Buying a car could take up a few hours of your time so you must not buy a car when you are tired. It is a considerable investment and can turn into a nightmare if you end up with something you do not really like. However, there is no greater feeling than driving your new car home knowing that you did all you could to find the best deal in town.

Exercise 2.36: Identifying Types of Pronouns (HB pp. 51–53)

For each underlined pronoun, write the correct number (1–7) to classify its type. One has

1. subject pronoun 2. object pronoun 3. relative pronoun	4. indefinite pronoun 5. reflexive pronoun	6. demonstrative pronoun 7. possessive pronoun

1. Our cookies are good, but <u>theirs</u> are better.   _7_

2. <u>We</u> were invited to his graduation.   _____

3. Not those, <u>these</u> are for sale.   _____

4. I bought <u>her</u> a lovely birthday present.   _____

5. Help <u>yourself</u>; there is more in the fridge.   _____

6. Do you know <u>who</u> that is?   _____

7. Surprisingly, <u>he</u> was not ready.   _____

8. There is <u>someone</u> at the door.   _____

9. Say hi next time you see <u>him</u>.   _____

10. They needed help. They could not carry that heavy couch by <u>themselves</u>.   _____

11. The book <u>which</u> I am reading is great.   _____

12. I like <u>this</u> a lot. Let's get it.   _____

13. <u>Everyone</u> interested should attend.   _____

14. Don't take their water. <u>Ours</u> is in the car.   _____

15. The disease is spreading. <u>No one</u> is safe.   _____

16. I don't know the person <u>that</u> lives there.   _____

17. Write your essay! It won't write <u>itself</u>.   _____

18. Give <u>me</u> that flower vase, please.   _____

19. <u>This</u> is a great story.   _____

20. <u>It</u> is fun to spend time with friends.   _____

been done for you as an example.

Exercise 2.37: Identifying Types of Pronouns (HB pp. 51–53)

Find and underline all pronouns in these sentences. Then identify the type of pronoun by writing the number 1–7 above it. Look for 1. subject, 2. object, 3. relative, 4. indefinite, 5. reflexive, 6. demonstrative, and 7. possessive pronouns. The number at the end of each group of sentences indicates how many pronouns there are.

1. Joan is trying to figure out the fate of her new dress. She does not like it very much, but at the same time, she does not want to return it to the store either. (4)

2. My brothers told me that I would not be able to move all the furniture by myself, and they were right. This kind of task was just too much for me to take on. (5)

3. Michael had to borrow his sister's books because he lost his, so he started making a list of books to buy for his home library. (3)

4. Nothing is cheap these days. Our economy is in trouble. Every trip to the grocery store makes me wonder how much longer this will last. (3)

5. When you start something new, it is hard to know what will come out of it. (5)

Exercise 2.38: Identifying Types of Adjectives (HB pp. 53–55)

For each underlined adjective, write the correct number (1–5) to classify its type. One has

1. article 2. possessive adjective	3. demonstrative adjective 4. quantity adjective	5. descriptive adjective

1. This skirt is just what I need. ___3___
2. Many children are placed in daycare. _____
3. Sam has a new job. _____
4. I don't like apples. Do you have a banana? _____
5. What a lovely today it is. _____
6. I borrowed his dictionary for a day. _____
7. I met a few friends at the mall. _____
8. This is the best movie I have ever seen. _____
9. He lives in that house with the green roof. _____
10. I saw an interesting program last night. _____

11. Can you open the door, please? _____
12. Those are my shoes. Where are yours? _____
13. "Much Ado about Nothing" is a fun play to watch. _____
14. Their car is still outside. They have not left yet. _____
15. Flying is not cheap these days. _____
16. I love red roses. _____
17. A little money is all that you need. _____
18. I doubt her boss will be pleased. _____
19. Those children are all alone. _____
20. I have a brand new Cadillac. _____

been done for you as an example.

Exercise 2.39: Sequence of Adjectives (HB pp. 54–55)

Put the given adjectives in the correct sequencing order to define a noun in each group. One has been done for you as an example.

1. blue / old / dollhouse / plastic / a (an)
   an old blue plastic dollhouse

2. tiny / Japanese / paper / six / multi-colored / frogs
   _____

3. a(an) / small / table / antique / wooden
   _____

4. a / silver / shiny / pendant / Russian / 19th-century
   _____

5. new / a / round / ball / rubber
   _____

Exercise 2.40: Identifying and Editing Errors with Adjectives (HB pp. 53–55)

1. misplacement after nouns	3. wrong comparative form
2. making adjectives plural	4. lack of adjective ending

In each sentence, find an ELL mistake in the adjective usage and correct it. Identify what kind of ELL mistake it is.

1. _____ It is very snow in Canada in the winter. The scenery is beautiful.
2. _____ This is a history moment. The population in the U.S. has surpassed 300 million.
3. _____ Simon Bolivar has done a lot of things good for many countries in South America.
4. _____ She brought a lot of beautifuls clothes with her from Brazil.
5. _____ This car is more bigger than my old one.
6. _____ Trying to avoid that situation dangerous, she got into her car and drove away.
7. _____ There is an interest movie in the theater. Would you like to see it?
8. _____ What a great thing it is to go to DisneyWorld, the park most exciting in the world.
9. _____ It is more better to live in Florida than in Arizona. It is not as hot.
10. _____ Those paintings are very nices. You are very talented.
11. _____ Jane and Brian have been engaged for six months, and they are finally getting marry.
12. _____ I have taken a lot of greats trips in my life. The last one was to China.

Exercise 2.41: Identifying Types of Adjectives (HB pp. 53–55)

Find and underline 12 articles, 4 possessive adjectives, and 16 descriptive adjectives in this joke. Write ART, POSS, or DESC to indicate the type of adjective.

After years of delivering pizzas, selling shoes, and waiting tables, a young businessman had saved enough money to start his own business. He rented a beautiful office and got the best decorations that he could for his new place. Sitting there, he saw a man come into the outer office. The businessman wanted to look busy, as if his office were really doing well, so he picked up the phone and started to pretend that he was working on a big international deal. He was shouting incredibly huge figures and making giant proposals to buy and trade stocks. The second guy just stood there. He couldn't help overhearing everything.

Finally, the businessman hung up and asked the silent visitor, "Can I help you?" The rather timid visitor said, "Sure. I'm here to install your new phone."

Exercise 2.42: Identifying the Function of Adverbs (HB pp. 55–56)

Decide if the adverb in each sentence is modifying a verb (V), an adjective (ADJ), or another adverb (ADV). Write the part of speech in the space provided.

1. _____ My friend John <u>almost</u> never opens a book and therefore frequently fails tests.
2. _____ Many women agree that George Clooney is an <u>extremely</u> handsome man.
3. _____ Everyone knew that you would <u>quickly</u> complete the swimming portion of the race.
4. _____ She drove as <u>fast</u> as she could to make it to class on time.
5. _____ He knew that getting her parents to like him is going to be a <u>particularly</u> difficult task.
6. _____ I like how your stylist takes care of your hair. He does it <u>very</u> well.
7. _____ We were late to the airport, but the taxi driver got us there <u>unbelievably</u> fast.
8. _____ I <u>greatly</u> appreciated all the help I got when I first moved to this state.
9. _____ Unfortunately, his company profits have decreased <u>dramatically</u> this quarter.
10. _____ Moving to a new country is never easy. Getting used to new food is <u>especially</u> hard.

Exercise 2.43: Identifying the Function of Adverbs (HB pp. 55–56)

Circle the single-word adverb in each sentence, and then write *how, when, where, how often,* or *how much* to indicate which question the adverb is answering.

1. _____ He never misses a single concert of his favorite rock band.
2. _____ Complete this job application in blue or black ink and return it here to be considered for the job.
3. _____ They quickly realized that they had taken the wrong turn.
4. _____ We are planning to go to the beach tomorrow. Do you want to join us?
5. _____ Our last quiz was tricky, but today's seemed equally complicated.
6. _____ The new computerized format of the exam is designed so that the first nine questions are not so difficult, but few people can answer all nine of them.
7. _____ Most of the voters were quite dissatisfied with the new government plan.
8. _____ It is a fact that she and I used to be best friends, but our company had a very different atmosphere then. Under our current policy, friendships at work are not encouraged.

Exercise 2.44: Identifying Three Types of Adverbs (HB p. 56)

For each underlined adverb, write the correct number (1–3) to classify its type. One has been done for you as an example.

1. manner	2. frequency	3. degree

1. Mike drove <u>faster</u> than ever before.   *1*
2. They <u>rarely</u> go out to eat.   _____
3. He drank his coffee <u>slowly</u>.   _____
4. She <u>hardly</u> ever comes late to class.   _____
5. Jan has <u>always</u> loved cheesecake.   _____
6. She <u>gracefully</u> exited the taxi.   _____
7. Running late, they <u>almost</u> missed the train.   _____
8. We are <u>always</u> helping others.   _____
9. He <u>openly</u> criticized his boss.   _____
10. I think my life would be <u>completely</u> different had I not met my wife.   _____

11. Tom will <u>never</u> go on a cruise again.   _____
12. <u>Sometimes</u> it is nice to relax.   _____
13. Jim was <u>too</u> busy to answer the phone.   _____
14. <u>Patiently</u>, he waited for her to finish eating.   _____
15. Wonderful job! <u>Nicely</u> done!   _____
16. She is a <u>very</u> jealous person.   _____
17. She <u>usually</u> calls if she is running late.   _____
18. <u>Seldom</u> does anyone survive motorcycle accidents.   _____
19. No one doubts that he is <u>absolutely</u> insane.   _____
20. Don't try so <u>hard</u> to please him.   _____

Exercise 2.45: Identifying ELL Errors with Adverbs (HB pp. 55–56)

In each sentence, find an ELL mistake in adverb usage and correct it. Identify what kind of ELL mistake it is.

1. lack of adverb ending	4. underuse of advanced adverbs of degree
2. misplacement of adverbs	5. use of *much* and *very much* in affirmative
3. wrong adverb forms	statements

1. _____ This car is such a clever designed vehicle. I wish I owned one.

2. _____ The teacher asked quickly the students for their exam papers.

3. _____ He was my best friend, and I will forget him never.

4. _____ Many movie stars donate money, travel to poor countries, and provide very much assistance to the less fortunate.

5. _____ On the exam, the first question was the most challenging. The student responded to the question difficulty.

6. _____ She watches TV very much.

7. _____ I would like to thank you very very much for everything you have done for my family.

8. _____ I already have done my homework for tomorrow, so I can watch TV now.

9. _____ I need to pass this exam much so I could be promoted.

10. _____ I have rare seen my family since I moved to the United States.

11. _____ Tony always is willing to help a person in need. He is a wonderful person.

12. _____ A marathon is an extreme difficult Olympic event. Only people who train tirelessly have a shot at winning.

13. _____ My favorite sport is football. I like it much.

14. _____ After the hurricane, his house was uninhabitable utterly.

15. _____ The teacher made sure that all students understood the lesson after she had carefullnessly explained it.

Exercise 2.46: Identifying the Function of Conjunctions (HB pp. 57–58)

Indicate whether the conjunction in boldface is connecting phrases (P) or clauses (C). Write your answer in the space provided.

1. _____ I could drink anything right now, but a glass of water **or** orange juice would be nice.

2. _____ I looked under the bed **and** on the kitchen table, but I could not find my keys.

3. _____ They would have come to his birthday **if** they had not been out of town that day.

4. _____ **As soon as** she got home, she went straight to bed.

5. _____ Who could have known that she would be so poor **but** happy after he left?

6. _____ The weather was not at all good, **but** we drove to our cousin's house.

7. _____ He went straight home **after** his team won the match.

8. _____ If you want to have fun **or** gamble a little, Las Vegas is a great place to visit.

9. _____ He could never make it on time **even though** he knew it drove her crazy.

10. _____ Amy was getting sick, **so** she made an appointment with her doctor.

11. _____ My sister visited me two years ago, **and** we spent a wonderful month together.

12. _____ Julie was talking on the phone **while** she was driving to her yoga class.

Exercise 2.47: Identifying ELL Errors with Conjunctions (HB pp. 57–58)

Write the numbers (1–3) to identify each underlined conjunction. One has been done for you as an example.

1. coordinating	2. subordinating	3. correlative

1. She was a good student, <u>for</u> she always did her homework. __*1*__

2. You can pick <u>either</u> a white <u>or</u> blue shirt. Both look good on you. _____

3. They had a great house on a lake, <u>and</u> we were often invited for dinner. _____

4. <u>After</u> I graduated from college, I spent a year traveling in Europe. _____

5. He knew the shortest way to get to the station <u>as</u> he had lived in this town for 3 years. _____

6. I failed the test, <u>so</u> I had to stay home and study. _____

7. I like <u>neither</u> tea <u>nor</u> coffee. I prefer water. _____

8. <u>Not only</u> did he finish high school at 16, <u>but also</u> he was accepted to Yale. _____

9. <u>Although</u> Jill was only going 5 miles over the speed limit, she still got a ticket. _____

10. We won't be able to pay rent <u>unless</u> you get another job. _____

11. They could get there by bus <u>or</u> rent a car. _____

12. I would have been there for you <u>if</u> I had known that you needed my help. _____

13. <u>Both</u> Scott <u>and</u> Anna graduated from the same university. _____

14. <u>Once</u> he gets home, all he wants to do is watch TV. _____

15. My cousin <u>neither</u> goes to the gym <u>nor</u> exercises at home. He is lazy. _____

16. He was in a bad mood, <u>but</u> I knew that taking him out for dinner would cheer him up. _____

17. I have lived in Chicago <u>since</u> my family moved there in 2000. _____

18. I enjoy <u>both</u> beading <u>and</u> sewing in my spare time. _____

19. Joe did not do well on his test, <u>nor</u> was he sorry about it. _____

20. I love cold weather, <u>yet</u> I live in Florida. _____

Exercise 2.48: Identifying ELL Errors with Conjunctions (HB pp. 57–58)

In each sentence, find an ELL mistake in the conjunction usage and correct it. Identify what kind of ELL mistake it is.

1. lack of conjunction 2. lack of punctuation	3. extra conjunction 4. fragment

1. _____ I knew that my sister always wanted to visit the Grand Canyon, this year I booked a trip for both of us.

2. _____ Unfortunately, after living in India for several years and seeing the poverty.

3. _____ Everyone knows that Chris is a good father but he continues to spoil his children. He buys them anything they want.

4. _____ Because you are so brave, and you entered the water even though you knew that there might be sharks in it. You are my hero.

5. _____ She likes to go shopping; but however, her brother hates it.

6. _____ If I am unable to make an appointment to see the doctor tomorrow I will have to take a day off work to do it.

7. _____ Because the weather is extremely cold most of the year.

8. _____ Because it was raining we did not go to the beach.

9. _____ I knew that my dad was right about Tom, but because I was stubborn I continued seeing him.

10. _____ Because Larry was so tall, so it was very difficult for him to fit in the seat at the arena.

11. _____ Although Kate took that highway everyday and knew exactly how to get home.

12. _____ We did not have to get a taxi to get to the airport. Because one of the people I was traveling with decided to drive his car to the airport and leave it there.

13. _____ Even though I did all I could to help my friend study for her math test, but she failed it anyway.

14. _____ Jack came back from the soccer field all dirty so his mother sent him straight to the bathroom to take a shower.

15. _____ She was late, we missed the beginning of the film and found it difficult to understand what was going on.

Exercise 2.49: Identifying Types of Conjunctions (HB p. 58)

Find and underline all conjunctions in the following paragraph. Indicate whether they are 1. coordinating (6), 2. subordinating (2), or 3. correlative (4). Mark them accordingly. (Numbers in parenthesis indicate the number of each type.)

Although both ESL and EFL students are learning English, those who teach English to non-native speakers know that methods used in ESL classrooms are not always suitable for EFL ones. In her article, Mary Black explained how ESL methodology is adapted to EFL environment at the Institute of North American Studies (INAS) in Barcelona, Spain, where strong emphasis is made on sharing information orally and less on written communication. At INAS, classes are focused on listening and speaking because students can do reading and writing in the form of either journals or movie reports for homework. EFL students are not exposed to correct English as much as ESL learners are, so it is imperative that they learn correct grammar. Teachers provide explicit grammar instruction, check comprehension, and reinforce structure acquisition with clear board work. Students not only have written output but also practice speaking. Finally, Black pointed out the importance of communication and grammar combination. Grammar activities should be both communicative and focused on structure learning as well.

Exercise 2.50: Identifying Types of Prepositions (HB pp. 59–61)

Write L, T, or M above each preposition to indicate if it is a preposition of location (L), time (T), or movement (M).

1. I wonder why we decided to meet at Jim's house at 8 PM on Saturday. It is so early.

2. Yesterday I did a bit of driving at night. After dinner, we had to drop Jane at her house. From her house, I drove five miles to Rick's apartment and then finally home.

3. I do not like going to movie theaters. Sometimes if you miss the beginning of a movie you want to see by 20 minutes, you have to wait for two hours. Renting movies is my thing.

4. After the reception, Chris invited us to go to his house to celebrate the end of the project he has been working on for the past three months.

5. I got a gift on Valentine's Day with a little note attached, which read: With all my love, from my heart to yours.

Exercise 2.51: Identifying and Editing ELL Errors with Prepositions (HB pp. 59–61)

In each sentence, find an ELL mistake in the preposition usage and correct it. Identify what kind of ELL mistake it is.

1. confusion of *at/on/in* with times 2. confusion of *at/on/in* with places 3. lack of prepositions	4. extra prepositions 5. wrong prepositions

1. _____ There were several kinds of snacks at last night's party, including to cheese and pretzels.

2. _____ When I was little, we would always go to my grandparents' house on August and eat as much watermelon as we could.

3. _____ Some people do not like to listen music. I always have my MP3 player with me.

4. _____ Have you seen the mess on her car? She has shoes on her dashboard, and there are potato chips on the floor.

5. _____ His speech made an impression to everyone who heard it.

6. _____ My parents lived at Caracas all their life before moving to Florida.

7. _____ Criminals who commit crimes do so regardless the circumstances.

8. _____ When I was growing up, I was completely dependent of my parents.

9. _____ Some singers put their hearts on their songs, and people appreciate that.

10. _____ John graduated from high school at 2005 but decided to wait a year before applying to colleges.

11. _____ Every morning before work, Jill drops her daughter off on Little Book Academy.

12. _____ There are a dozen of reasons to support the government's plan.

13. _____ I hate my grammar class. We always have tests in Mondays. Why can't our teacher change them to Tuesdays?

14. _____ Do you believe for ghosts?

15. _____ You have helped us so much that we would like to give you this gift certificate to thank you all your help during the past three years.

Exercise 2.52. Identifying Prepositional Phrases (HB pp. 59–61)

In the following text on error correction, put parentheses around the 12 prepositional phrases. Remember that infinitives (*to* + base form of the verb: to *go*) are not prepositional phrases.

Correction is an issue of concern for ESL and EFL teachers. Considerable research has been done in the past decades on the subject. Some researchers believe that learners should be free to produce typical overgeneralization errors for L2 structures. Others state that the lack of correction might imply to the learner that an incorrect production is correct. They believe correction is necessary at some point in a learner's L2 development. Many researchers agree that if students recognize that they are making errors, it should help them realize that they need to continue their learning. There is no doubt that to benefit from correction, learners need to know that they are being corrected. Immediate correction allows students to notice the difference between their version of the L2 and correct production.

Exercise 2.53: Changeable Parts of Speech: Form vs. Function (HB pp. 62–63)

Indicate whether each boldface word is used as a noun (N), a verb (V), or an adjective (Adj).

1a. ____	I **water** plants twice a week.	1b. ____	I am thirsty. Do you have any **water**?	1c. ____	I love Monet's **water** lilies.
2a. ____	He is **speaking** in front of friends.	2b. ____	I had **speaking** difficulties when I was a child.	2c. ____	Public **speaking** is an art form.
3a. ____	She often goes to **plant** exhibits.	3b. ____	They **plant** a tree in the yard every spring.	3c. ____	Which **plant** should I grow in this spot?
4a. ____	She won't quit without a **fight**.	4b. ____	Have you seen "**Fight** Club"?	4c. ____	He could **fight** better than I could.
5a. ____	This suitcase is so **light**.	5b. ____	Could you give me some **light**?	5c. ____	Fireworks **light** up the sky every 4ᵗʰ of July.

Exercise 2.54: Changeable Parts of Speech: Form vs. Function (HB pp. 62–63)

In Items 1–3, write a short sentence using the word as a noun, a verb, and an adjective. One has been done for you as an example. In Items 4 and 5, write original words used as a noun, a verb, and an adjective.

Word	Noun	Verb	Adjective
1. bread	I like bread.	I breaded the meat.	There was a bread shortage.
2. bike			
3. star			
4.			
5.			

Exercise 2.55: Review Parts of Speech (HB pp. 40–63)

In this short text on "staycations," write the part of speech above each of the 20 underlined words. Use these abbreviations: noun N, verb V, adjective Adj, adverb Adv, preposition Prep, pronoun Pro, conjunction Conj.

It is now ①clear that the ②rising cost of gasoline has had a tremendous effect on the price of ③almost everything else. Families used to take vacations ④every summer. They'd hop in their cars and drive hours and sometimes a day or two to reach their ⑤destination. With the prohibitive cost of gasoline now, many families are opting for "staycations" instead of vacations.

A ⑥staycation is an innovative ⑦way to enjoy some time away from work and school. Instead of ⑧traveling elsewhere to visit a museum or a park, families are ⑨now exploring similar ⑩sites in their own cities. People are spending their vacations doing things ⑪within a very short driving distance of their own homes.

⑫Many people don't use all of their ⑬paid vacation ⑭because they are afraid they will get ⑮too behind in their work ⑯if they actually take all of their ⑰allocated vacation days. Others don't have the funds to use up all of their vacation days. A staycation is a good way for these workers to take a ⑱break without ⑲breaking the bank. After all, ⑳everyone needs a few days away from the usual routine.

Exercise 2.56: Review Parts of Speech (HB pp. 40–63)

In this brief literature review on cooperative learning, write the part of speech above each of the 20 underlined words.

Cooperative (1) learning is an (2) instructional technique that (3) has been shown to increase academic achievement (4) and prosocial development (Blaney, et al., 1977; Marr, 1997). Marr (1997) (5) recommended introducing group work (6) gradually beginning (7) with brief, straightforward tasks and increasing to more complex and (8) demanding tasks (9) as the groups refine (10) their abilities to work (11) collaboratively. Blaney et al. (1977) (12) conducted a field (13) study with 5th grade students who spent three class periods (14) per week for six weeks in small (15) interdependent learning groups. Students in experimental groups demonstrated more friendliness (16) toward group members. They also increased (17) self-esteem and (18) decreased competitive (19) behavior. Furthermore, they viewed their classmates as resources, not (20) merely as persons to compete against.

Exercise 2.57: Review Parts of Speech: Creating a Cinquain Poem (HB pp. 40–63)

A cinquain is a five-line poem. The word *cinquain* comes from the French word *cinq*, which means "five." Your task is to use the correct parts of speech to create an original cinquain. After you have finished, take turns reading other students' cinquains.
There are many variations of cinquains, but one format of a cinquain is as follows:

Line 1 / one word: a single noun (the title of the cinquain)
Line 2 / two words: two adjectives that describe Line 1
Line 3 / three words: three –ing verbs that are actions that Line 1 might do
Line 4 / four words: a phrase or sentence that reveals a feeling related to Line 1
Line 5 / one word: a single noun that summarizes or renames Line 1

Example:

Cats
Aloof, curious
Sleeping, hiding, purring
A friendly ball of fur
Kitty

Your cinquain:

_____

_____

_____

_____

_____

PRACTICE FOR SECTION 3:
Basic Grammar Labels for Sentence Structure

Exercise 2.58: Identifying Subjects and Predicates (HB pp. 64–65)

For each sentence, draw a line to separate the subject from the predicate.

1. The style of reading in Renaissance Europe is deftly charted in this welcome volume from Anthony Grafton.

2. Growing out of the Thomas Spencer Jerome Lectures that Anthony Grafton gave at the University of Michigan in 1992, this book describes the interaction between books and readers in the Renaissance.

3. Humanists Alberti, Pico, Budé, and Kepler, all major figures of their time and now major figures in intellectual history, are examined in the light of their distinctive ways of reading.

4. Investigating a period of two centuries, Grafton vividly portrays the ways in which book/scholar interactions were part of and helped shape the subjects' Humanistic philosophy.

5. The book also indicates how these traditions have implications for the modern literary scene.

6. *Commerce with the Classics: Ancient Books and Renaissance Readers* illustrates the immense variety of the humanist readers of the Renaissance.

7. Grafton describes life in the Renaissance library, how the act of reading was shaped by the physical environment, and various styles of reading during the time.

8. A strong sense of what skilled reading was like in the past is built up through anecdotes, philological analysis, and documents from a wide variety of sources.

Exercise 2.59: Identifying Simple Subjects and Simple Predicates (HB pp. 64–65)

In the text about a book, underline the simple subject with one line and the simple predicate with two lines. Draw a line to separate the complete subject from the complete predicate in each clause.

Each chapter of the revised edition of *The Article Book* includes presentation of a rule with examples, exercises, quizzes, and a comprehensive test. While the 50 rules are taught to provide a logical framework for the text and serve as a handy reference, students will learn through guided practice instead of memorization. *The Article Book* may serve as either a supplement to any ESL/EFL core text or as a self-study tool for intermediate through advanced learners. *Fish Trek* is a well-designed interactive computer game created specifically to help teach English article usage. It offers six game levels, ten levels of difficulty, and a comprehensive practice session. Feedback is tailored to the question and not the generic "right" or "wrong." A plus for teachers is the test generator feature. While *Fish Trek* software supports *The Article Book*, the book and the software can be used separately.

Exercise 2.60: Direct and Indirect Objects (HB p. 65)

Decide whether the underlined word is a direct (DO) or indirect object (IO) in each sentence. Write the symbols above each underlined noun.

1. Wendy wrote each wedding <u>guest</u> a personal thank you <u>note</u>.

2. Ann gave <u>James</u> the <u>instructions</u> on how to bake <u>banana bread</u>.

3. Children are thrilled when they get <u>gifts</u> on their birthday.

4. Thank <u>you</u> so much. We really appreciate your generous <u>contribution</u>.

5. Richard wanted a <u>computer</u>, and his parents got <u>him</u> <u>one</u> last December.

6. Every time I watch "<u>The Godfather</u>," I am amazed how talented all of the actors in that movie are.

7. When summer comes, kids love to go to the beach and build <u>sand castles</u>.

8. I have read all six <u>novels</u> written by Jane Austen. I truly enjoyed <u>them</u>.

9. Every night before bed time, Rita read her <u>granddaughter</u> a few <u>stories</u>.

10. My parents just celebrated their 30th wedding <u>anniversary</u>, and we got <u>them</u> a <u>trip</u> for two to California's wine country.

Exercise 2.61: Transitive and Intransitive Verbs (HB pp. 65–66)

Identify each underlined verb as transitive (VT) or intransitive (VI). Remember that some verbs may change their usage depending on the context.

___ ___ 1. When Joshua <u>broke</u> his mother's favorite salad bowl, he <u>felt</u> very sad.

___ ___ 2. When kids <u>climb</u> trees, they rarely <u>think</u> about the danger of falling.

___ ___ 3. Even through the organizers <u>cancelled</u> the show, none of us <u>complained</u>
___   because they <u>gave</u> us our money back.

___ 4. Every Thanksgiving my mother <u>prepares</u> her famous stuffing and gravy
        from scratch.

___ ___ 5. Homeowners <u>received</u> the letters that <u>contained</u> information about
        possible home insurance increases.

___ ___ 6. Nancy <u>received</u> a special treatment at the spa that <u>consisted</u> of a full body
        massage as well as a facial.

___ ___ 7. As soon as Jason <u>walked</u> into the room, everyone <u>knew</u> whose son he
___ ___   <u>was</u> because he greatly <u>resembled</u> his father.

___ 8. Due to an accident that <u>happened</u> a week earlier, Andrew was unable
___ ___   to <u>travel</u> to his hometown for Christmas because he <u>spent</u> 10 days in the
        hospital.

___ 9. Mike <u>brought</u> his girlfriend a lovely bouquet of roses.

___ 10. Whenever something unexpected and potentially dangerous <u>occurs</u>,
___ ___   some people <u>perform</u> better while others <u>fail</u>.

Exercise 2.62: Transitive and Intransitive Verbs (HB pp. 65–66)

In the following text, label each underlined verb as transitive (VT) or intransitive (VI). Remember that some verbs may change their usage depending on the context.

A man ① walked ( ) down the street to the bus stop. A woman ② was sitting ( ) on the bench. She ③ was reading ( ) a newspaper, and a small dog ④ was lying ( ) on the sidewalk in front of her. As the man ⑤ sat ( ) down on the bench beside her, the woman ⑥ looked ( ) up at him over the newspaper, and the man ⑦ smiled ( ). The woman ⑧ started ( ) reading the newspaper again. After a few minutes, he ⑨ asked ( ) the woman, "Does your dog ⑩ bite ( )?" The woman ⑪ turned ( ) the page in the newspaper and ⑫ answered ( ), "No."

The man ⑬ reached ( ) down and ⑭ petted ( ) the dog, and the dog ⑮ bit ( ) him. The man ⑯ jumped ( ) away from the dog and ⑰ shouted ( ) at the woman, " I ⑱ thought ( ) that you ⑲ said ( ) your dog ⑳ didn't bite ( )!" The woman ㉑ turned ( ) another page of the newspaper. Then she ㉒ paused ( ), ㉓ looked ( ) directly up at the man, and ㉔ answered ( ), "㉕ That's ( ) not my dog."

Exercise 2.63: Student Errors with Transitive and Intransitive Verbs (HB pp. 65–66)

Find ELL errors related to transitive and intransitive verbs in each sentence. Underline and correct them. Put a check mark (✓) in the correct column to indicate the type of error.

1. The direct object is left out or inserted where it is not necessary.
2. An unnecessary preposition is inserted.
3. An incorrect preposition is inserted.
4. The preposition is omitted.

	1	2	3	4
1. My brother likes to listen good music.				
2. I have always depended at my family to take care of me.				
3. Many people enjoyed at the party Maria had at her house.				
4. Maria went shopping for shoes and bought in the mall.				
5. I look forward going to my friend's birthday party.				
6. She waited to him for a long time, but he never came.				
7. Something bad happened my car last week. I was very upset.				
8. I don't see your book. Where did you put?				
9. John was waiting for the letter and finally received.				
10. The class read *Great Expectations* and discussed about it.				
11. I got really surprised with his extraordinary voice.				
12. Josh Groban can make an impression to everyone who listens to his songs.				
13. I think he is a good singer, and I am so impressed about his voice.				
14. They could not come back home safely because good luck did not come them all the time.				

Exercise 2.64: Transitive and Intransitive Verbs (HB pp. 65–66)

Identify the usage of the underlined verb by writing VT if the verb is transitive and VI if it is intransitive. Carefully consider the context of each sentence.

		Verb Usage, VT or VI
1. The world leaders <u>focused</u> their attention on the most urgent problems.	2. Even though it was dark outside, Paul <u>focused</u> to see what was going on.	1. _____ 2._____
3. Jennifer may <u>enter</u> the university in May.	4. It is no secret that other considerations <u>enter</u> when money is involved.	3. _____ 4._____
5. Ann <u>spoke</u> to the issue of global warming at last week's conference.	6. No one liked it when Adam <u>spoke</u> his mind freely. Many thought he was wrong.	5. _____ 6._____

Exercise 2.65: Phrases (HB p. 67)

Use Numbers 1, 2, and 3 to label the type of underlined phrases. <u>Reminder</u>: A **phrase** is a group of words without a subject and a verb.

1 = noun phrase
2 = verb phrase
3 = prepositional phrase

1. _____ The Civil War started in Charleston, South Carolina, with the firing <u>on Fort Sumpter</u>.

2. _____ Established as the Carolina Art Association in 1858, the Gibbes Museum of Art <u>opened its doors to the public in 1905</u>.

3. _____ King Street is <u>Charleston's main street</u> and part of the original King's Highway into the city.

4. _____ Each year golfers flock to the Charleston area to play some <u>of the finest courses</u> in the world.

5. _____ On August 31, 1886, an earthquake estimated to measure 6.6 to 7.3 on the Richter Scale <u>hit Charleston</u>.

Exercise 2.66: Independent and Dependent Clauses (HB pp. 67–68)

Put parentheses around each clause in the following text. Write IC if the clause is independent and DC if it is dependent. There are five independent and three dependent clauses. Locating the verbs first will make the task easier.

Managing Readers explores the fascinating interchange between text and margin, authorship and readership in early modern England. William W. E. Slights considers overlooked evidence of the ways that early modern readers were instructed to process information, to contest opinions, and to make themselves into fully responsive consumers of texts. The recent revolution in the protocols of reading that was brought on by computer technology has forced questions about the nature of book-based knowledge in our global culture. *Managing Readers* traces changes in the protocols of annotation and directed reading from medieval religious manuscripts and Renaissance handbooks for explorers, rhetoricians, and politicians to the elegant clear-text editions of the Enlightenment and the hypertexts of our own time. The book contains twenty-two illustrations of pages from rare-book archives that immediately clarify the distinctive management of the reading experience during the first century-and-a-half of printing in England.

Exercise 2.67: Adverb Clasues (HB pp. 67–68)

Underline all the adverb clauses in the sentences. Circle subordinating conjunctions.

1. Although *Much Labouring* by David Holdeman will particularly interest students of modernism, the uncommon significance of Yeats's textual experiments suggests new perspectives on interpretive and editorial theories and practices generally.

2. While its principal appeal will be to students of Oscar Wilde and the Victorian fin-de-siècle, this book will also appeal to textual and literary scholars, art historians, and linguistic philosophers interested in the graphical nature of the linguistic sign.

3. Mark used to visit the Eiffel Tower every time he came to Paris because that place reminded him of the day he proposed to his wife.

4. I would have wanted to be a singer if I had not become a teacher. I had bright prospects when I was sixteen and even attended a preparatory course at the conservatory for a year.

5. John's sister loves sports cars whereas he prefers sturdier family models. They can never agree on the ideal car when they talk about cars.

Exercise 2.68: Adjective Clauses (HB pp. 67–68)

Underline all the adjective clauses in the sentences. Circle relative pronouns.

1. Knowledge is something that can not be bought. Education, on the other hand, is something that we pay for.

2. *Power and Possibility* is a collection of critical works by contemporary poets that gathers together articles, interviews, and book reviews.

3. Many ELL reading books contain prereading and comprehension questions as well as exercises that reinforce the vocabulary and idiomatic expressions.

4. Writing templates can enhance students' scores on standardized tests like the TOEFL® iBT and SAT® by providing them with a structure that conforms to grading criteria.

5. Educators know that students who are able to concentrate do better on standardized tests. There are specific strategies students can practice to improve their concentration ability.

Exercise 2.69: Noun Clauses (HB pp. 67–68)

Underline all noun clauses in the sentences. Circle the words that introduce noun clauses.

1. That living in New York is not going to be cheap was clear to Ian even before he moved there since he was coming back to the city where he had previously spent three years of his life.

2. *Oscar Wilde's Decorated Books* by Nicholas Frankel examines the role played by graphic designers in the production of Wilde's writings and demonstrates how marginal and decorative elements of the printed book affect interpretation.

3. James was in London when he found out that his father was hospitalized with a heart attack. He rushed back and hoped that he would be able to see his father alive.

4. I never remember how to get to my friend's house. I have been there several times already, but I cannot remember which exit I should take off the highway.

5. It is too late to decide whether he was right or wrong. By now, no one cares about what happened to him.

Exercise 2.70: Adverb, Adjective, and Noun Clauses (HB pp. 67–68)

Use numbers 1, 2, or 3 to identify each boldface clause. One has been done for you as an example.

1. adverb clause	2. adjective clause	3. noun clause

1. **Whenever Jane comes home,** she turns on the news.   _1_

2. I know **that telling the truth is the best policy.**   _____

3. **What I ate for lunch** made me sick.   _____

4. I was sick **because I overate.**   _____

5. She did not tell me **when she would call me.**   _____

6. The sofa **that I bought last week** is very comfortable.   _____

7. **Where Ann went** is a secret.   _____

8. No one knows **where he lives.**   _____

9. I forgot to ask **how long the movie runs.**   _____

10. The man **who sold me his car** moved to Arizona.   _____

11. Yesterday I ran into a friend **I had not seen in years.**   _____

12. He was prepared to move **whenever she asked him.**   _____

13. It is important **that you change the oil in your car regularly.**   _____

14. **What he said** made everyone upset.   _____

15. She said **she would be back at noon.**   _____

16. **Why they broke up** is a mystery even to their closest friends.   _____

17. She has spoken English well **since she moved to England.**   _____

18. I know **who took the last cookie.**   _____

19. I need a friend **whom I can trust.**   _____

20. **Even though he bought a house,** he has not moved in yet.   _____

Exercise 2.71: Types of Sentences (HB pp. 69–70)

Use numbers 1, 2, 3, or 4 to identify each sentence. One has been done for you as an example.

1 = simple
2 = compound
3 = complex
4 = compound-complex

1. Whenever Jane comes home, she turns on the news.   _3_

2. It may be fun to just sit on the beach, look at the sky, and do nothing.   _____

3. I don't like coffee, but I can't live without tea.   _____

4. Do not drink and drive, but if you do drink, try to find a designated driver.   _____

5. Coffee has caffeine while most green teas do not.   _____

6. When you are in New York, you should visit my aunt, and don't forget to watch a Broadway musical.   _____

7. Where the treasure lies is unknown.   _____

8. Salt is used all over the world, and it is no secret that in the old days it was valued very highly.   _____

9. We had a choice to go to the movies, or we could stay home and watch a rental.   _____

10. Close that door, please!   _____

11. Driving and skating are her two favorite pastimes in the world.   _____

12. Maria knew how to get there, yet no one asked her opinion.   _____

13. They liked the neighborhood, so they bought a house there.   _____

14. As part of the triathlon, he swam, ran, and rode a bike.   _____

15. They were having a picnic, and when it started to rain, they decided to go back home.   _____

16. It is important that you change the oil in your car regularly.   _____

17. If you want things done right, do them yourself, or you could ask for your friend's help.   _____

18. I help my sister with her English homework, and she helps me with my math.   _____

19. My father and I used to go fishing and hunting every summer.   _____

20. The sofa that I bought last week is very comfortable.   _____

Exercise 2.72: Subject-Verb Agreement (HB p. 71)

Circle the correct form of the verb to complete each sentence.

1. Either the Chief Executive Officer or the Vice President (is, are) going to make that decision.

2. Unfortunately, some of the people (seems, seem) to disagree with this decision.

3. Everyone accepted to one of the universities (has, have) to provide medical records and vaccination history.

4. Tonight is the final of the soccer tournament, so the captain along with the players (is, are) nervous.

5. All of the books including the ones left on reserve (was, were) picked up by the students.

6. Would you like a slice of pie? Some of it (is, are) still in the fridge.

7. Tony (lives, live) in such a dangerous part of town that when something (happens, happen), even the police (does, do) not want to get involved.

8. The amount of gasoline annually used in the United States alone (is, are) staggering.

9. The news of ethanol's popularity in South America (is, are) spreading around the world making consumers interested and thus driving up its price.

10. It (was, were) natural disasters that caused the most damage around the world in 2004–2005, not humankind.

11. It is not the faculty members but rather the president of the university who (decides, decide) the issue.

12. When the new semester started, it became apparent that some of the books (was, were) missing from the library.

13. After the storm, neither of the traffic signals on the park street (was, were) working.

14. Even after visiting the company's website, some hiring criteria (was, were) still not clear to Bob.

Exercise 2.73: Sentence Composition Errors (HB pp. 71–73)

Identify the underlined sentence composition errors as F (fragment), RO (run-on), or CS (comma splice), and then correct them. Corrections may vary.

1. <u>A terrible earthquake struck China many</u> people lost their lives. International aid came from all over the world.

2. <u>With gas prices going up, some people are buying more fuel-efficient cars, others</u> are trying to slow down so they can get better mileage.

3. <u>The professional engineering exam is one of the hardest tests that engineers will have to take in their lives, I suggest</u> you start studying for it as soon as possible.

4. <u>I did not know which ice cream flavor to pick I was</u> too tempted to get a few different ones.

5. <u>I had been dreaming about visiting Spain for a long time, finally, I got</u> a chance to do this last year when I flew to Madrid and spent two weeks there.

6. <u>Even before the Thanksgiving weekend and certainly weeks before Christmas.</u>

7. <u>The students did not intend to cause any damage or harm they</u> were simply dressed in scary costumes for Halloween.

8. He would watch any show even if he had seen it a million times <u>before, she preferred to read</u>.

9. <u>Because none of the answers for the first question on the exam seemed plausible.</u> Many students were confused and missed subsequent items.

10. The recipe takes four hours to prepare. <u>Is very complicated.</u> The ingredients are not cheap.

Exercise 2.74: Sentence Composition Errors (HB pp. 71–73)

Find sentence composition errors by marking F (fragment), RO (run-on), or CS (comma splice), and then correct them. Corrections may vary.

1. _____ Even though he was an experienced politician running for President and had some great ideas to improve the country's health care system.

2. _____ The mess that the children created in their room was not easy to clean up, I gave up after an hour.

3. _____ The skater started the program slowly. Then she started landing difficult jumps, the audience gave her a standing ovation at the end of her performance.

4. _____ There is no doubt that Prohibition was necessary at the time, it was not very popular among alcohol producers.

5. _____ If I had known that that meeting was going to be the last time that I would ever see her.

6. _____ Some of the students wanting to travel to France in the summer and spend a month living with host-families and learning the language.

7. _____ It is amazing how many people sell things online these days some make it their daily jobs.

8. _____ My sister decided to change a career after working as a business analyst for more than ten years the family is 100 percent behind her decision.

9. _____ Troubled by rising gas prices and concerned about the instability of the global economy.

10. _____ The Browns decided to redecorate their home office. Jeannette cleaned the carpet and chose the paint, Rob painted the wall.

11. _____ This next section of the movie has a lot of interesting details and information necessary for the understanding of the plot, watch it carefully.

12. _____ Organic food is becoming very popular, many people are willing to spend a bit more on it even though the benefits of eating organic produce have not been fully researched yet.

13. _____ Thank you for inviting me over for dinner Saturday night however I am unable to make it as it also happens to be my sister's birthday that day.

14. _____ My friend has been importing medical equipment, in fact he imports three million dollars worth of equipment every quarter.

15. _____ Practicing tirelessly her answers to the sample interview questions and adding final touches to her resume.

PRACTICE FOR SECTION 4:
Why the Twelve English Verb Tenses Matter

Exercise 2.75: Four Principal Parts of a Verb (HB pp. 74–75, 336–340)

Fill in the missing principal parts for these 15 verbs.

Base (Simple)	Present Participle	Past	Past Participle
1.	calling		
2. speak			
3.			delayed
4.	taking		
5.		went	
6.	flying		
7.		put	
8.			cried
9.		ate	
10. cut			
11.			visited
12. cringe			
13.		had	
14.			worn
15. open			

Exercise 2.76: Four Principal Parts of a Verb (HB pp. 74–75, 336–340)

Put a check mark (✓) by each of the principal parts that each verb form given could represent. Note that each verb form may have multiple answers possible. One has been done for you as an example.

1. *moved* __ simple (base) __ present participle ✓ past ✓ past participle	2. *say* __ simple (base) __ present participle __ past __ past participle	3. *worked* __ simple (base) __ present participle __ past __ past participle	4. *preparing* __ simple (base) __ present participle __ past __ past participle
5. *read* __ simple (base) __ present participle __ past __ past participle	6. *taken* __ simple (base) __ present participle __ past __ past participle	7. *come* __ simple (base) __ present participle __ past __ past participle	8. *forgiving* __ simple (base) __ present participle __ past __ past participle
9. *wanted* __ simple (base) __ present participle __ past __ past participle	10. *cut* __ simple (base) __ present participle __ past __ past participle	11. *went* __ simple (base) __ present participle __ past __ past participle	12. *lost* __ simple (base) __ present participle __ past __ past participle

Exercise 2.77: Simple Present Tense (HB p. 76)

Conjugate the regular verb *take* and the irregular verb *be* in the affirmative, negative, and interrogative. (For 2.77–2.88, use one pronoun as an example for your answers in the center and right columns.)

	Affirmative	**Negative**	**Interrogative**
take	I/you/we/they *take*	I *do not take*	*do I take?*
	he/she/it		
be	I		
	you/we/they		
	he/she/it		

Exercise 2.78: Simple Past Tense (HB p. 76)

Conjugate the regular verb *work* and the irregular verb *take* in the affirmative, negative, and interrogative.

	Affirmative	**Negative**	**Interrogative**
work	I/you/we/they *worked*		
	he/she/it		
take	I/you/we/they		
	he/she/it		

Exercise 2.79: Simple Future Tense (HB p. 77)

Conjugate the verb *go* in the affirmative, negative, and interrogative.

	Affirmative	**Negative**	**Interrogative**
go	I/you/we/they *will go*		
	he/she/it		

Exercise 2.80: Present Progressive Tense (HB p. 77)

Conjugate the verbs *work* and *put* in the affirmative, negative, and interrogative.

	Affirmative	**Negative**	**Interrogative**
work	I *am working*		
	you/we/they		
	he/she/it		
put	I		
	you/we/they		
	he/she/it		

Exercise 2.81: Past Progressive Tense (HB p. 78)

Conjugate the verbs *open* and *begin* in the affirmative, negative, and interrogative.

		Affirmative	Negative	Interrogative
open	I *was opening*		
	you/we/they			
	he/she/it			
begin	I			
	you/we/they			
	he/she/it			

Exercise 2.82: Future Progressive Tense (HB p. 78)

Conjugate the verbs *take* and *wait* in the affirmative, negative, and interrogative.

		Affirmative	Negative	Interrogative
take	I/you/we/they *will be taking*		
	he/she/it			
wait	I/you/we/they			
	he/she/it			

Exercise 2.83: Present Perfect Tense (HB p. 79)

Conjugate the verbs *work* and *be* in the affirmative, negative, and interrogative.

		Affirmative	Negative	Interrogative
work	I/you/we/they *have worked*		
	he/she/it			
be	I/you/we/they			
	he/she/it			

Exercise 2.84: Past Perfect Tense (HB p. 80)

Conjugate the verbs *work* and *have* in the affirmative, negative, and interrogative.

		Affirmative	Negative	Interrogative
work	I/you/we/they *had worked*			
	he/she/it			
have	I/you/we/they			
	he/she/it			

Exercise 2.85: Future Perfect Tense (HB p. 80)

Conjugate the verbs *work* and *go* in the affirmative, negative, and interrogative.

		Affirmative	Negative	Interrogative
work	I/you/we/they *will have worked*			
	he/she/it			
go	I/you/we/they			
	he/she/it			

Exercise 2.86: Present Perfect Progressive Tense (HB p. 81)

Conjugate the verbs *take* and *check* in the affirmative, negative, and interrogative.

		Affirmative	Negative	Interrogative
take	I/you/we/they *will have been taking*			
	he/she/it			
check	I/you/we/they			
	he/she/it			

Exercise 2.87: Past Perfect Progressive Tense (HB p. 82)

Conjugate the verbs *take* and *do* in the affirmative, negative, and interrogative.

		Affirmative	**Negative**	**Interrogative**
take	I/you/we/they	*had been taking*		
	he/she/it			
do	I/you/we/they			
	he/she/it			

Exercise 2.88: Future Perfect Progressive Tense (HB p. 83)

Conjugate the verbs *take* and *work* in the affirmative, negative, and interrogative.

		Affirmative	**Negative**	**Interrogative**
take	I/you/we/they	*will have been taking*		
	he/she/it			
work	I/you/we/they			
	he/she/it			

Exercise 2.89: Identifying Verb Tenses in English (HB pp. 74–85)

Match the examples with their correct verb tense by writing the correct letter next to the corresponding example.

Example	*Verb Tense*
1. ___ we will design	a. simple present tense
2. ___ we were designing	b. simple past tense
3. ___ we will have been designing	c. simple future tense
4. ___ we had designed	d. present progressive tense
5. ___ we have been designing	e. past progressive tense
6. ___ we will be designing	f. future progressive tense
7. ___ we design	g. present perfect tense
8. ___ we designed	h. past perfect tense
9. ___ we had been designing	i. future perfect tense
10. ___ we have designed	j. present perfect progressive tense
11. ___ we are designing	k. past perfect progressive tense
12. ___ we will have designed	l. future perfect progressive tense

Exercise 2.90: Identifying Verb Tenses in English (HB pp. 74–85)

Conjugate the verbs *choose* and *recycle* in all 12 tenses. Where all forms are the same (e.g., past tense), list the one form: *chose*. Where forms vary (e.g., present progressive), list all possible forms: *am/is/are choosing*.

Verb Tense	*Choose*	*Recycle*
simple present	1.	2.
simple past	3.	4.
simple future	5.	6.
present progressive	7.	8.
past progressive	9.	10.
future progressive	11.	12.
present perfect	13.	14.
past perfect	15.	16.
future perfect	17.	18.
present perfect progressive	19.	20.
past perfect progressive	21.	22.
future perfect progressive	23.	24.

Exercise 2.91: Identifying Verb Tenses in English (HB pp. 74–85)

Place a check mark (✓) by each verb phrase that is labeled with the correct verb tense.

___ 1. *reacts* = simple present	___ 26. *is deciding* = present perfect
___ 2. *had harmed* = past perfect	___ 27. *has been running* = present progressive
___ 3. *has been* = present perfect progressive	___ 28. *had gone* = past perfect
___ 4. *had been saying* = past progressive	___ 29. *will have asked* = future perfect progressive
___ 5. *have done* = present perfect	___ 30. *had been asking* = past progressive
___ 6. *will necessitate* = simple future	___ 31. *has been going* = present perfect progressive
___ 7. *take* = simple past	___ 32. *are withdrawing* = present progressive
___ 8. *am looking* = present progressive	___ 33. *had been taking* = past perfect
___ 9. *had been organizing* = past perfect progressive	___ 34. *is considering* = present progressive
___ 10. *has been eating* = present perfect	___ 35. *has been thinking* = present perfect progressive
___ 11. *will have taken* = future perfect	___ 36. *will have chosen* = future perfect
___ 12. *had been trying* = past progressive	___ 37. *had attempted* = past progressive
___ 13. *had eloped* = past perfect	___ 38. *have needed* = present perfect
___ 14. *will have been living* = future progressive	___ 39. *were systematizing* = past perfect progressive
___ 15. *has* = simple present	___ 40. *are attempting* = present perfect
___ 16. *will have been sitting* = future perfect progressive	___ 41. *will be watching* = future progressive
___ 17. *was working* = simple past	___ 42. *had had* = past perfect
___ 18. *will have seen* = present perfect	___ 43. *had needed* = simple past
___ 19. *will decide* = simple future	___ 44. *have comprehended* = present perfect
___ 20. *has been* = present progressive	___ 45. *standardize* = simple present
___ 21. *were cooking* = past progressive	___ 46. *will be eating* = future progressive
___ 22. *have been going* = present perfect progressive	___ 47. *are building* = present progressive
___ 23. *has investigated* = future perfect	___ 48. *handed* = simple past
___ 24. *had been urging* = past perfect	___ 49. *has* = present perfect
___ 25. *has been working* = present progressive	___ 50. *had been reporting* = past progressive

Exercise 2.92: Identifying Verb Tenses in English (HB pp. 74–85)

Place a check mark (✓) by each verb phrase that is labeled with the correct verb tense.

___ 1. *was lending* = simple past	___ 26. *had had* = past perfect
___ 2. *has precipitated* = present progressive	___ 27. *centralize* = simple present
___ 3. *had gone* = past perfect	___ 28. *has been dropping* = present progressive
___ 4. *had been reporting* = past progressive	___ 29. *will have painted* = future perfect progressive
___ 5. *have placated* = present perfect	___ 30. *had been demanding* = past progressive
___ 6. *proposed* = simple present	___ 31. *is picking* = present perfect
___ 7. *were chopping* = past progressive	___ 32. *will be farming* = future progressive
___ 8. *have been culling* = present perfect progressive	___ 33. *are retracting* = present progressive
___ 9. *has depicted* = present perfect progressive	___ 34. *had lain* = past perfect
___ 10. *had been having* = past perfect progressive	___ 35. *is being* = present progressive
___ 11. *had been sorting* = past progressive	___ 36. *had perpetuated* = past progressive
___ 12. *are inciting* = present perfect	___ 37. *had set* = simple past
___ 13. *has developed* = future perfect	___ 38. *tabled* = simple past
___ 14. *had taught* = past perfect	___ 39. *have praised* = present perfect
___ 15. *was learning* = simple past	___ 40. *are repelling* = present progressive
___ 16. *will have been occupying* = future progressive	___ 41. *were assuaging* = past perfect progressive
___ 17. *will have flown* = future perfect progressive	___ 42. *will be watching* = future progressive
___ 18. *has been dreaming* = present progressive	___ 43. *had been exacerbated* = past progressive
___ 19. *will require* = simple future	___ 44. *has been going* = present perfect progressive
___ 20. *had been cajoling* = past perfect	___ 45. *mitigated* = present perfect
___ 21. *has been eating* = present perfect	___ 46. *has been taking* = present perfect progressive
___ 22. *will puzzle* = simple future	___ 47. *have rescinded* = present perfect
___ 23. *will have wavered* = future perfect	___ 48. *will have chosen* = future perfect
___ 24. *behoove* = simple present	___ 49. *are blocking* = present perfect
___ 25. *are drawing* = present progressive	___ 50. *had been facilitating* = past perfect

Exercise 2.93: Perceptions of Verb Tense Usage in the Real World (HB pp. 74–85)

English has 12 verb tenses, but they are not used equally. Tenses such as present progressive and simple past are used more frequently than future perfect progressive or past perfect. In addition, verb tenses are not used randomly. ELLs and teachers need to be aware that certain types of language situations tend to make use of certain verb tenses. Knowing which verb tenses your ELLs will encounter most frequently can inform your grammar instruction.

Which verb tense(s) do you expect to find in the following language situations? Give reasons for your answers. Discuss your answers with colleagues. What do you agree on? What do you disagree on?

Language Situation	Your Predictions
1. a conversation involving a study group of three students (about a math assignment) (Exercise 2.94)	Verb tense(s):
	Your rationale:
2. a written excerpt of the survivor of a severe hurricane (from a historical book) (Exercise 2.95)	Verb tense(s):
	Your rationale:
3. a written excerpt from an encyclopedia article on animals such as giraffes or elephants (Exercise 2.96)	Verb tense(s):
	Your rationale:

Exercise 2.94: Perceptions of Verb Tense Usage in the Conversations of Native Speakers (HB pp. 74–85)

Corpus linguistics examines the language that people really use—as opposed to what textbooks prescribe that we should say. We can verify the language that people actually use by analyzing a corpus, which is a large body or collection of actual language data. A corpus may consist of written work such as newspaper articles or novels, spoken work such as transcripts of conversations or lectures, or both written and spoken language.

With modern computer technology, building a corpus and analyzing the language in it have led to a better understanding of real language usage. One such corpus is the Michigan Corpus of Academic Spoken English, or MICASE. The MICASE corpus is a spoken language corpus of approximately 1.8 million words (200 hours) focusing on contemporary university speech within the University of Michigan. This university is a typical large public research institution with about 41,000 students, approximately one-third of whom are graduate students. Speakers represented in the corpus include faculty, staff, and all levels of students, and both native and non-native speakers.

The following transcript contains an excerpt involving three (native-speaking) students in a math study group. Underline all of the verbs, and write the tense above. Count the total number of verbs and then the number of verbs by verb tense. Based on the total number of all verbs, calculate the percentage of usage for each verb tense. Record your data in the chart.

Finally, how do these figures compare with your prediction from Exercise 2.93? (IMPORTANT: For this exercise, omit modal verbs such as *can, might, must,* and *should* as well as imperatives or commands such as *let me just point* and *show that.*)

	Simple	Progressive	Perfect	Perfect Progressive	TOTALS
Present	__ / __%	__ / __%	__ / __%	__ / __%	__ / __%
Past	__ / __%	__ / __%	__ / __%	__ / __%	__ / __%
Future	__ / __%	__ / __%	__ / __%	__ / __%	__ / __%
TOTALS	__ / __%	__ / __%	__ / __%	__ / __%	__ /100%

Title: Math Study Group
Transcript ID: SGR385SU057
Publisher: MICASE, English Language Institute, University of Michigan
Number of Participants: 3
Recording Date: March 27, 1999
Approximate Word Count: 700

S1: All right, is the Moebius transformation stuff in here or is it in the, Stahl, or is it not in anything?

S2: Um, I don't know I shoulda brought my notebook.

S1: I don't see Moebius in here. . . .

S3: Is that the handout?

S1: Yeah, this was that co—this was conjugacy so, it might not have anything to do with Moebius.

S3: Okay.

S2: I think it must be in Stahl like on around page one-fifty-nine, 'cuz that's what our exercises are out of.

S3: Does she spell Moebius wrong? She spells it M O B I U S.

S1: Well, no, she puts [S2: Yeah] M O with the two, dots above it.

S2: With the two dots just like she does in the book.

S1: I think she spells it right [S2: Yeah] like let me just point to where (he's) wrong.

S2: It's like Moebius. I can't say it like she can. She's like Moebius.

S3: You know, I have like this other teacher in, four-fifty, and she was spelled it like, M O E B I U S.

S2: That's how they spell it in the book.

S3: I know. But, in our other class like four-thirty-three, spelled it like, Natasha. So I don't know what's right.

S1: All right, so . . . .

S2: I think, O E is a linguistic form it's a vowel, and it goes like /oe/ it goes however she says Moebius, it goes like that, and it's an actual vowel in linguistics and so i think that's why they spell it like that.

S1: All right, so what's R-hat?

S3: And so does the [S2: R-hat] O-dot-dot replace the [S1: Is that like] O-E or something?

S2: Yeah.

S3: Okay.

S1: Is that like [S2: I think] R minus infinity?

S2: I'm trying to remember if it's R minus infinity or R minus zero or . . .

S1: Or R no maybe it's R union with infinity.

S2: Plus infinity yeah because C-hat is, the complex numbers union infinity.

S1: Right, so that must be what it is. Okay?

S2: All right so, show that, given any three points X Y and Z in R-hat, there is a Moebius transformation which sends the points zero one and infinity to X Y and Z respectively.

S1: Okay so, we wanna find a . . . Moebius transformation . . . *<PAUSE:10>* zero to, minus one to Y infinity to Z.

S2: So don't we do it like she was doing 'em in class?

S3: Was this on Friday or, when?

S2: Um, I don't know she just seemed to do something like this, one we want to go to Y, and infinity we want to go to Z. So then we have to write 'em, F-of-Z equals equals F-of-X, right isn't that what we do? F-of-X equals and now we want it to be, zero, A plus zero all over, zero, B plus zero?

S1: So we're n—there's no complex numbers in this so that's kinda weird. 'Cuz the Moebius, I thought, okay well Z doesn't have to be a complex number it can be a real number cuz real numbers are complex numbers? [S3: Yeah] Okay. [S2: Yeah] All right.

S2: So, F-of-X equals, actually we only need A to be zero right? Doesn't matter [S1: So, you want] what everything else is.

S1: So you want F of-zero to equal X. Is that what we're saying? Equal X.

S2: Um, oops yeah.

S1: Right. So, it doesn't matter what A is right? And it doesn't matter what C is. It just mat—and D can't equal zero. Right?

S2: Well, we have to have, one of 'em be X.

S1: Oh right.

S3: So.

S2: So, we want A to be one right? So it'll be one-X, so we want [S3: Yeah, that's] A to equal one, B to equal zero, C to equal zero and D [S3: B to equal zero, C to equal zero, and D] to equal one.

S1: Oh, but here's, here's what the p—but we're supposed to, we're mapping zero to X so isn't, you stick zero in for Z right? [S2: Uhuh] not X. [S2: Right] So you wanna make, you wanna make [S3: You wanna make] B X. You know what I'm saying?

Exercise 2.95: Perceptions of Verb Tense Usage about a Past Event (HB pp. 74–75)

The following excerpt is from *Category 5: The Story of Camille, Lessons Unlearned from America's Most Violent Hurricane*, a book detailing the terrible story of Hurricane Camille of 1969. Underline all of the verbs, and write the tense above. Count the total number of verbs and then the number of verbs by verb tense. Based on the total number of all verbs, calculate the percentage of usage for each verb tense. Record your data in the chart.

Finally, how do these figures compare with your prediction from Exercise 2.93? (IMPORTANT: For this exercise, omit modals as well as imperatives or commands.)

	Simple	Progressive	Perfect	Perfect Progressive	TOTALS
Present	__ / __%	__ / __%	__ / __%	__ / __%	__ / __%
Past	__ / __%	__ / __%	__ / __%	__ / __%	__ / __%
Future	__ / __%	__ / __%	__ / __%	__ / __%	__ / __%
TOTALS	__ / __%	__ / __%	__ / __%	__ / __%	__ /100%

Hurricane Camille struck the coast of southern Mississippi hard on the evening of August 17, 1969, killing 259 people in its wake. A handful of remarkable survival tales emerged, including that of 33-year old Mary Ann Gerlach, who gained near-instant national fame with her astonishing survival story. She and her sixth husband, Frederick (or "Fritz," as most people knew him), had lived at the Richelieu Apartments. Both had worked night shifts the evening before the hurricane, she as a waitress and he as a Seabee in the Navy. Mary Ann told reporters:

> The first thing that popped into my mind was party time! We all got together and decided we were going to have a hurricane party on the third floor. I went out and got all kinds of stuff to fix, you know, sandwiches and hors d'oeuvres. Well, all the Civil Defense people had come up trying to get us out, and the manager and his wife kept telling us, "There's no need to go. It's ridiculous, so just stay here."

Mary Ann and Fritz never did join the group on the third floor. They decided to nap first, but thumping sounds from below awakened them around 10:00 PM. The electricity was out by then, and they ventured into the living room by flashlight. To their horror, the Gulf of Mexico was one-third of the way up their second-story picture window, some twenty feet above normal sea level. As they dashed back to their bedroom, the front window imploded, the sea rushed in, and the building shuddered. Their only option now was to get ready to swim. Unfortunately, years earlier as a new enlistee, Fritz had talked a buddy into passing his swimming test for him, and now that ruse came back to haunt him since he didn't know how to swim at all. With waist-deep water swirling around them and their furniture floating, Mary Ann blew up an air mattress that she kept for the swimming pool and gave it to Fritz.

Moments later, the rear window shattered and she swam out with the current—smack into a maze of electrical wires. The sea, surging in through the front and out the rear of the apartment, swept Fritz out behind her. She disentangled herself and pushed off from the doomed building. "My legs," she explained, "were real strong, you know, from doing waitress work for so long." Meanwhile, Fritz drowned. Several days later, his body was found tangled in a tree several miles inland.

Some six hours later, unable to walk and wearing only tattered shorts and the ragged remnants of a short-sleeved sweatshirt, Mary Ann sat shivering in the mud into the morning. She spied a man tramping through the debris and called to him for help. He asked if she had seen his wife. "No, I haven't seen anyone alive but you," she replied. The man stumbled away in a trance, repeating his wife's name over and over.

She huddled, still shivering, for more than an hour before the next person came along, a young man she recognized as a local post office clerk. She called out to him. The postal clerk and the two other men carried Mary Ann to a high school, where school officials were converting one area of the school to a temporary morgue and most of the rest of the building was sheltering survivors. A few hours later, several National Guard troops transferred her to the Miramar Nursing Home. There, as her wounds were being tended, Mary Ann explained to the nurses that she was the sole survivor of the Richelieu Apartments.

The word quickly got out to the reporters, and as journalists swarmed in to interview her over and again, Mary Ann got better and better at remembering various details of her extraordinary survival story. Nationwide, hundreds of broadcasts and newspapers reported that Mary Ann Gerlach had been the sole survivor out of two dozen revelers at a "hurricane party" in the ill-fated apartment building.

In truth, at least eight others had survived the destruction of the Richelieu. Several of them had heroic motives for remaining there that terrible night, and all suffered consequences as agonizing as Mary Ann's harrowing experience. Camille's "hurricane party," however, has become embedded in American folklore, and perhaps some good has come from that. Wittingly or not, Mary Ann Gerlach raised the consciousness of millions of Americans that hurricanes are not auspicious occasions for partying.

Exercise 2.96: Perceptions of Verb Tense Usage in a Scientific Article (HB pp. 74–85)

For this activity, use the Internet to locate a generic article about an animal (e.g., elephant, giraffe, or tiger). Your instructor may wish to assign an animal to you to demonstrate that verb tense usage for any particular type of writing is fairly consistent. Identify all of the verbs and write the tense above. Count the total number of verbs and then the number of verbs by verb tense. Based on the total number of all verbs, calculate the percentage of usage for each verb tense. Record your data in the chart. (IMPORTANT: Do not include modals or imperatives in your counts.)

Finally, how do these figures compare with your prediction from Exercise 2.93?

	Simple	Progressive	Perfect	Perfect Progressive	TOTALS
Present	__ / __%	__ / __%	__ / __%	__ / __%	__ / __%
Past	__ / __%	__ / __%	__ / __%	__ / __%	__ / __%
Future	__ / __%	__ / __%	__ / __%	__ / __%	__ / __%
TOTALS	__ / __%	__ / __%	__ / __%	__ / __%	__ /100%

❖❖❖ 3 ❖❖❖

15 Keys to ELL Grammar

ELL Grammar Key 1: to be (HB pp. 90–99)

3.1.1. What are the eight forms of the verb *to be* in English?

simple/base: _____

present: _____, _____, _____

past: _____, _____

present participle: _____

past participle: _____

3.1.2. Can you identify and explain these common ELL errors with this grammar point? Match the number of the type of error with its example.

Errors with *be*

1. Do not use **am**, **is**, or **are** with the wrong subject.
2. Do not omit **am**, **is**, or **are** from the sentence.
3. Do not use **have** for **be** with these words: *hungry, thirsty, right, wrong, sleepy, tired, lucky, . . . years old.*
4. Do not forget to include the subject.

Student Errors

_____ a. My favorite sports are baseball and football. I think are great games for everyone.

_____ b. I like Mrs. Henson's class. My friend and I am happy there.

_____ c. Now I have 22 years old.

_____ d. All the people in my family very tall like me.

_____ e. This newspaper published in English and Spanish.

_____ f. Guatemala City is very big. Is not located near the sea.

_____ g. In my country, there many men with moustaches.

_____ h. If he has right, then he can talk to her about the situation.

3.1.3. What are some similarities in the forms of *be* in simple present tense and simple past tense?

3.1.4. Negating verbs in English is not an easy task (e.g., *I go* → *I don't go, I could* → *I couldn't,* and *you took* → *you didn't take*). However, negating *to be* is easy. How do you negate the verb *to be* in English?

3.1.5. Are contractions with *be* possible in both simple present tense and simple past tense? If not, explain.

_____

_____

3.1.6. What is one effect of using contractions in spoken language that ELLs should be made aware of?

_____

_____

3.1.7. Forming yes-no questions in English is often difficult because it requires the use of auxiliary verbs (e.g., *she likes* → *does she like*). Explain how to form yes-no questions with *to be*.

_____

_____

_____

3.1.8. Explain how to form *wh-* questions with *to be*.

_____

_____

_____

_____

3.1.9. Find the eight errors with verb *to be* in this student writing.

> This is a map of North America. The country to the north of the United States are Canada. Canada a very large country, but not so many people live in Canada. The population are 29,000,000. The leaders in Canada want more people to come to live in their country. I think they have right because Canada needs more people.
>
> Canada has two official languages. These two languages is English and French. Most of the people who speak French live in Quebec. Quebec are a large province in Canada. The capital of Canada is Ottawa. The largest cities is Toronto, Vancouver, and Montreal. Vancouver is in the west, but Toronto and Montreal is not in the west. Montreal is in the eastern part of the country, and Toronto is in the central part of Canada.

Action Research Project to Inform Your Teaching

Ask students of different first languages to translate these six sentences into their native languages:

1. I am not from Canada.

2. He is 40 years old.

3. I am a teacher.

4. He is a teacher.

5. I am at the bank now.

6. I am eating now.

Compare the forms of *be* for these six sentences. What differences are there with English in terms of the verb *to be*?

ELL Grammar Key 2: *Verb Tenses to Express Present Time* (HB pp. 100–113)

3.2.1. Much of the time, the tense of a verb in English logically matches the time of the action. However, there is sometimes a difference between the time of an action and the verb tense that is used to express it. Give an example.

_____

_____

_____

_____

3.2.2. Fill the chart with examples of the verb tense usages that match the meanings.

Verb Tense	Example	Present Meaning
Simple Present		a habitual or repeating action
Present Progressive		a current action
Present Perfect		an action that began in the past but continues to be true
Present Perfect Progressive		an action that began in the past but is continuing now (with emphasis on the fact that it is still happening)

3.2.3. Should teachers and textbooks focus on simple present tense first and then go on to present progressive, or should these two be covered in reverse order? What are the pros and cons for each of these two sequences?

_____

_____

_____

_____

_____

_____

3.2.4. What are the two forms of the verb *take* in simple present tense? _____, _____

3.2.5. In simple present tense, most verbs simply add –*s* to form the third person singular. Give two rules of irregular spelling. Include two examples for each.

a. _____

_____

_____

b. _____

_____

_____

3.2.6. What are the three forms of the verb *take* in present progressive tense?

_____, _____, _____

3.2.7. What is the rule for doubling or not doubling the final consonant when creating the present participle form?

_____

_____

_____

_____

_____

3.2.8. Can you identify and explain these common ELL errors with this grammar point? Match the number of the type of error with its example.

Errors with Present Progressive Tense

1. Don't use VERB or VERB + –s for actions that are happening just now or only once.
2. Don't use –ing for actions that happen every day or all the time.
3. Don't forget to use **be.**
4. Be careful with the spelling of the present participle.
5. Don't use present progressive if the verb does not show an action (as opposed to a state of being).

Student Errors

_____ a. *The cook preparing the dinner for tonight's special occasion.*

_____ b. *She can't hear you because she is listenning to her loud music.*

_____ c. *About ninety percent of U.S. households are owning a car now.*

_____ d. *In the election today, most of the city's residents voting by computer.*

_____ e. *The sun is rising in the east, and the morning light is so beautiful.*

_____ f. *Look out! A car comes from the left!*

_____ g. *We are busy now. I am cuting the meat, and she is making the salad.*

_____ h. *On a postcard: We are enjoying Hawaii very much. We are having a great time here. We are having a great hotel room. We are eating excellent food.*

_____ i. *Excuse me, but do you know if anyone sitting in this chair?*

_____ j. *Please wait here. Susan drives here from her house right now.*

3.2.9. What are the two forms of the verb *take* in present perfect tense?

_____, _____

3.2.10. How do you form the past participle of regular verbs?

_____

_____

_____

3.2.11. Are the rules for doubling or not doubling the final consonant before adding *–ed* the same as those before adding *–ing?* If not, list any important differences.

_____

_____

_____

3.2.12. How do you form the past participle of irregular verbs?

_____

_____

_____

_____

_____

_____

3.2.13. Can you identify and explain these common ELL errors with this grammar point? Match the number of the type of error with its example.

Errors with Present Perfect Tense

1. Do not forget to use **have** or **has** with the past participle for an action that began in the past and still continues.
2. Do not use **have** or **has** with the wrong subject.
3. Do not forget to use the past participle with present perfect tense.

Student Errors

_____ a. *The total cost have now reached $1,000, so the boss must approve any additional money.*

_____ b. *Since 2007, more women than men have enter major universities.*

_____ c. *From 2007 until now, about 80 percent of applicants passed their driver's license exam on their first attempt.*

_____ d. *The principal has already finish writing the final reports.*

_____ e. *So far I traveled to 22 countries. I plan to go to two more this month.*

_____ f. *As a result of the recent news, the members of the committee has agreed to call off the current construction project.*

_____ g. *In this decade, many people have purchase modern computers.*

_____ h. *Ahmed worked here for ten years. He likes this job very much.*

3.2.14. What are the two forms of the verb *take* in present perfect progressive tense?

_____ , _____

3.2.15. Can you identify and explain these common ELL errors with this grammar point? Match the number of the type of error with its example.

Errors with Present Perfect Progressive Tense

1. Do not forget to use **have** or **has** with **been** followed by the present participle.
2. Do not use present progressive tense for an on-going action (even though it is happening in present time).

Student Errors

_____ a. *We been waiting for a taxi for more than ten minutes already.*

_____ b. *It is raining since noon. I wonder when it will stop.*

_____ c. *Mrs. James is a great customer. She is coming to our café since we opened in 2000.*

_____ d. *Our university is fully computerized now. In fact, our office of admissions is using an online admissions application since 2005. There are no more paper forms.*

_____ e. *Most airlines are in severe economic trouble. Many been losing money for many years, but somehow they continue to fly passengers.*

3.2.16. How do you form the negative of these verb tenses?

Tense	Negative Form
Simple Present	
Present Progressive	
Present Perfect	
Present Perfect Progressive	

3.2.17. Of the four tenses for expressing present time, which is the most difficult for ELLs to negate? Why?

_____

_____

_____

_____

3.2.18. Can you identify and explain these common ELL errors with this grammar point? Match the number of the type of error with its example.

Errors with Negating

1. Do not forget to use **do not** or **does not** with simple present tense.

2. Do not use **am not, is not,** or **are not** with the base form of a verb. Use **do not** or **does not** only.

3. With simple present tense, do not use –s with the verb for **he/she/it.** You need an –s for **he/she/it** only one time in the verb. If you have **does,** then the verb cannot have an –s, too.

4. Do not use **don't, doesn't,** or **didn't** to negate verbs in present perfect or present perfect tenses. Don't confuse **don't have** with **haven't.** Don't confuse **doesn't have** with **hasn't.**

Student Errors

_____ a. Unlike Chile, Bolivia does not haves a seacoast.

_____ b. Many of the people in this country not possess a passport.

_____ c. Professional tennis players today are not take many vacation days.

_____ d. I love sweets, but my brother doesn't likes them at all.

_____ e. They think the new plan is good, but the boss does not agrees with them.

_____ f. Many people not speak English well. They need English classes immediately.

_____ g. We don't have lived here very long, but we like the area very much.

_____ h. If he does not have had much experience with international sales jobs, then he should not apply for the job because they want someone with international experience.

3.2.19. Complete this chart with the possible contractions.

Verb Tense	Affirmative	Negative
Simple Present		
Present Progressive		
Present Perfect		
Present Perfect Progressive		

3.2.20. What is the rule for when the word *has* can and cannot be contracted to *'s*?

_____

_____

_____

_____

3.2.21. Of the four tenses we have been studying (simple present, present progressive, present perfect, and present perfect progressive), which one or ones do you think is the hardest for ELLs to use correctly in the negative form? Why?

_____

_____

_____

_____

_____

_____

3.2.22. Can you identify and explain these common ELL errors with this grammar point? Match the number of the type of error with its example.

Errors with Forming Questions

1. For simple present tense, remember to use **does** with **he, she,** and **it** in questions and negatives. Use **do** with other subjects.

2. For simple present tense, do not put **–s** on the verb in questions and negatives. Use only the base (simple) form of the verb. For **he/she/it,** you need only one **–s** in the question.

3. Do not begin simple present tense verb questions with **am, is,** or **are** unless the main verb is *to be.*

4. For questions using present progressive, begin with **am, is,** or **are,** not **do** or **does.**

5. Do not use **do, does,** or **did** in question form of present perfect tense.

Student Errors

_____ a. How many miles of seacoast do Chile have?

_____ b. When does Flight 227 from New York arrives in Dubai?

_____ c. Are you like spaghetti or rice more?

_____ d. Where do you living now?

_____ e. How long do you have lived here in Buenos Aires?

_____ f. To open a new account, this bank does not requires a letter of recommendation.

_____ g. Is the menu have anything for vegetarians on it?

_____ h. My school identification card does not says my real date of birth on it. How can I change this?

3.2.23. Find the eight errors with **present time** in this student writing.

> To sum up, cell phones are with us for a relatively short period of time, but they have already become an extremely important mode of communication. Over time, people have been more attracted to this amazing little device. The result now is that almost everyone is owning a cell phone. In fact, some people has multiple cell phones. Although it is a popular way to communicate, cell phones has many negative impacts on people. Some people really aren't like to use cell phones, and their reasons for avoiding them is very convincing. A cell phone is a disruptive instrument and often endangers people's lives. In my opinion, the negative aspects of this tiny device outweighs the positive aspects by a wide margin.

 ## Action Research Project to Inform Your Teaching

Consult a content textbook such as science, health, business, or mathematics. Choose an excerpt of approximately 1,000 words in the middle of the textbook. Underline all of the verbs. In most content textbooks, we expect a high number of present tense verbs, but is this the case? Use a rubric with all twelve of the verb tenses to see which tenses are represented and to what extent? (Calculate percentages when you have finished labeling and tallying the verbs.)

ELL Grammar Key 3: *Verb Tenses to Express Past Time* (HB pp. 114–137)

3.3.1. There are five verb tenses and two special verb expressions that express some aspect of past time. Complete this chart with original examples of these verb tenses and verb expressions.

Verb Tense / Expression	Past Meaning	Example
Simple Past Tense	a single past event	
Past Progressive Tense	a past action that was happening (when it was interrupted by another)	
Present Perfect Tense	a past action (indefinite time) that could happen again	
Past Perfect Tense	a past action that was completed before a second past action	
Past Perfect Progressive Tense	an action that began in the past before a second past action (with emphasis on the duration of the action)	
Used to and *Would*	*Used to*: an action that happened many times in the past but is no longer true; frequently opens a past narrative *Would*: refers to smaller actions that happened repeatedly in a past narrative but are no longer true	

3.3.2. In simple present tense, verbs have two forms: VERB and VERB + –s. How many forms does a verb have in simple past tense? _____

3.3.3. What are the spelling rules when adding *–ed* for past tense?

_____

_____

_____

3.3.4. Give five examples of irregular verbs in simple past tense.

_____, _____, _____, _____, _____

3.3.5. Can you identify and explain these common ELL errors with this grammar point? Match the number of the type of error with its example.

Errors with Forming Questions

1. Don't use VERB or VERB + **–s** in the past tense. Don't forget to use **–ed**.
2. Do not use **was/were** with verbs (other than *to be*) in simple past tense (in active voice).
3. Don't forget to change **y** to **i** and add **–ed**.
4. If a verb ends in **consonant-vowel-consonant (C-V-C)** (in its stressed syllable), don't forget to double the consonant before adding **–ed**.

Student Errors

_____ a. *Two of the children carried the kittens to the car in a small box.*

_____ b. *The rising flood water traped several people in the cave.*

_____ c. *Yesterday I finally pass my driver's license test on my second attempt.*

_____ d. *Columbus set forth on his first journey on August 3, 1492. The three ships in his expedition was not have any soldiers on board because this was an exploratory trip.*

_____ e. *At the meeting last night, the two oldest people in our office were state their reasons for voting against the proposal.*

_____ f. *In college, I joined the soccer team, but the team was not that good. The players did not show up for practice, but they show up at game time. The coach did not know what to do.*

3.3.6. How many different forms does the verb *eat* have in past progressive tense? Write them here.

_____

3.3.7. Can you identify and explain these common ELL errors with this grammar point? Match the number of the type of error with its example.

Errors with Forming Questions

1. Do not use **was/were** + VERB without **–ing** to indicate simple past tense.
2. Don't mix up past progressive tense and simple past tense.
3. Be careful with the spelling of the present participle.
4. Don't use past progressive if the verb does not show an action (as opposed to a state of being).

Student Errors

_____ a. *We were liking the car so much that we decided there and then to buy it.*

_____ b. *Yesterday morning was a routine day for me. I was getting up at six. I took a shower. I left my house at seven.*

_____ c. *Around midnight last night, the phone was ringing once very loudly.*

_____ d. *What kind of reception for the guests were you planing for after the wedding?*

_____ e. *What time was United Airlines Flight #337 finally arrive?*

3.3.8. How many forms does the verb *work* have in present perfect tense? Write them here.

_____

3.3.9. How do you form the past participle for regular verbs?

_____

_____

3.3.10. How do you form the past participle for irregular verbs?

_____

_____

3.3.11. ELLs who see a list of past participle forms of irregular verbs may feel overwhelmed. What can a teacher tell these ELLs to lessen the apparent learning burden?

_____

_____

_____

_____

3.3.12. The *Keys to Teaching ELL Grammar Handbook* lists seven usages for present perfect tense. Fill in this chart with an original example for each usage and the important time words that often accompany each usage.

No.	Usage	Original Example	Key Words
1.	Past action or situation that continues now		
2.	Recent past action that is important to the current situation		
3.	Past experience, indefinite past time		
4.	With *yet* (indicates a past indefinite action)		
5.	With a superlative (indicates a past indefinite action)		
6.	Ordinal numbers (refers to a past indefinite time)		
7.	Repetition of an action before now (exact time is not important)		

3.3.13. Can you identify and explain these common ELL errors with this grammar point? Match the number of the type of error with its example.

Errors with Forming Questions

1. Do not forget to use **have** or **has** with the past participle.
2. Do not use **have** or **has** with the wrong subject.
3. Do not use **be** instead of **have** or **has** with present perfect tense.
4. Do not use present perfect with any specific past tense time words.
5. Do not use simple past tense with actions that are still continuing.

Student Errors

_____ a. *An astronaut has first landed on the moon in 1969.*

_____ b. *Can you tell me what time Flight 1334 has arrived in Los Angeles yesterday?*

_____ c. *Our teacher worked at this school since 2000. I hope I have her again next year.*

_____ d. *This intersection is very dangerous. Many accidents were happened here.*

_____ e. *The new cars from this company has been very popular with consumers.*

_____ f. *The blue line is the oldest train line in this city. In fact, I taken this line to and from work since 1990.*

_____ g. *We wrote six papers in this class so far. When will this work end?*

_____ h. *Yesterday's earthquake has caused the ground to shake violently for twenty seconds.*

3.3.14. How many forms does the verb *work* have in past perfect tense? Write them here.

_____

3.3.15. Can you identify and explain these common ELL errors with this grammar point? Match the number of the type of error with its example.

Errors with Verbs with Past Perfect

1. Do not forget to use the past participle after **had**.
2. Do not use past tense when past perfect is required.

Student Errors

_____ a. *By 1999, the company had file for bankruptcy twice already.*

_____ b. *By 1999, the company filed for bankruptcy twice already.*

_____ c. *I wish I had write a better letter to the family upon their grandson's death.*

_____ d. *If I saw him yesterday, I would have told him about your news.*

_____ e. *We entered the kitchen and were shocked at what we saw. There sat little Amanda covered in flour and oil. The kitchen was a disaster. Amanda cooked dinner.*

3.3.16. How many forms does the verb *work* have in past perfect progressive tense? Write them here.

_____

3.3.17. Can you identify and explain these common ELL errors with this grammar point? Match the number of the type of error with its example.

Errors with Past Perfect Progressive Tense

1. Do not forget to use **had** with **been** followed by the present participle.
2. Do not use past progressive tense for an on-going action.

Student Errors

_____ a. The weather was awful yesterday. In fact, when you arrived last night, it been raining for more than four hours straight.

_____ b. When I arrived, the kids were sleeping for two or three hours already, so I decided not to wake them up.

_____ c. When we walked into the kitchen, we were shocked at the site of Amanda sitting there covered in flour and oil. She was smiling. The kitchen was a disaster area. "I made bread," said little Amanda. Clearly, Amanda been cooking.

_____ d. When I saw Rob yesterday morning, he had bags under his eyes. He said that he been working all night long on a new project.

3.3.18. How many forms does the verb *work* have with the expression *used to*? Write them here.

_____

3.3.19. How many forms does the verb *work* have with the expression *would*? Write them here.

_____

3.3.20. Which meaning do *used to* and *would* share? Write an original example.

_____

_____

3.3.21. Which meaning does *used to* have that *would* does not? Write an original example.

_____

_____

3.3.22. Can you identify and explain these common ELL errors with this grammar point? Match the number of the type of error with its example.

Errors with *would* and *used to*

1. ELLs are unsure of these two structures, so they rarely use them.
2. Don't use **would** for non-actions.

Student Errors

_____ a. In the 1980s, I would be a university student majoring in French.

_____ b. Singapore would be part of Malaysia. However, this union lasted only from 1963 to 1965.

_____ c. In the 1990s, I taught in Saudi Arabia. We taught from 5 AM to 1 PM. We worked six days a week. I had classes on five days, and the students came to see me for additional help on the sixth day.

_____ d. When I was a young child, I remember that my grandfather would live on a small farm. He lived there until 1974, when he moved in with us.

_____ e. Life was different in the early 1900s. People shopped for their food daily because they didn't have any refrigerators. Compared to today's citizens, people exercised much more often then. Couples married at an earlier age.

3.3.23. How do you form the negative of these verb tenses?

Verb Tense/ Expression	Negative Form
Simple Past	
Past Progressive	
Present Perfect	
Past Perfect	
Past Perfect Progressive	
Used to	
Would	

3.3.24. Of the five tenses and two expressions for expressing past time, which is the most difficult for ELLs to negate? Why?

_____

_____

_____

3.3.25. What are three mistakes that ELLs routinely make with the negative form of simple past tense?

_____

_____

_____

3.3.26. Can you identify and explain these common ELL errors with this grammar point? Match the number of the type of error with its example.

Errors with Negating Past Tense Verbs

1. Do not forget to use **did not** with simple past tense.

2. For simple past tense, do not use **was not** or **were not**. Use **did not** only.

3. With simple past tense, do not use **–ed** with the verb. The auxiliary **did** means past, so you don't need another **–ed** to indicate past (again).

4. For past progressive, do not forget to use **was** or **were**.

5. Do not use **don't** or **doesn't** to negate verbs in present perfect tense. Don't confuse **don't have** with **haven't**. Don't confuse **doesn't have** with **hasn't**.

6. Do not use **didn't** to negate verbs in past perfect tense. Don't confuse **didn't have** with **hadn't**.

7. The negative of **used to** is **did + use to + VERB**. Do not write **used**.

Student Errors

_____ a. *The office that issues building permits doesn't have given me a permit to build a new roof on my garage.*

_____ b. *When I was a kid, I didn't used to like onions. Now I love them.*

_____ c. *He tried on the basketball shoes, but they not fit.*

_____ d. *My grades are not good. I don't have studied enough.*

_____ e. *I left the party early because I not having a good time.*

_____ f. *Luckily for everyone, the bad weather did not lasted very long.*

_____ g. *When we arrived at the airport, it didn't have snowed very hard yet.*

_____ h. *The steak dinner sounded good when the server described it, but I was not order it.*

3.3.27. Complete this chart with the possible contractions.

Verb Tense/ Expression	Affirmative	Negative
Simple Past		
Present Perfect		
Past Perfect		
Past Perfect Progressive		
Used to		
Would		

3.3.28. Complete this chart with the question forms of these verb tenses.

Tense	Question Form
Simple Past	
Past Progressive	
Present Perfect	
Past Perfect	
Past Perfect Progressive	
Used to	
Would	

3.3.29. Can you identify and explain these common ELL errors with this grammar point? Match the number of the type of error with its example.

Errors with Forming Questions with Past Tense Verbs

1. For simple past tense, do not put **–ed** on the verb. Use only the base (simple) form of the verb.
2. Do not begin simple past tense verb questions with **was** or **were**.
3. For questions with past progressive, begin with **was** or **were**, not **did**.
4. Do not use **did** in question form of present perfect tense.
5. Do not use **did** in question form in the past perfect tense.
6. In questions with **used to**, be sure to drop the **–d** in *used*.

Student Errors

_____ a. Someone told me that you live in Turkey now. How long did you live there?

_____ b. Did life in Latvia used to be very different before it joined the European Union?

_____ c. How much did she borrowed to buy that car?

_____ d. When you arrived at the hospital, were you see the doctor right away?

_____ e. At the meeting, how many people did wearing any kind of political campaign button?

_____ f. I'm glad your trip to Italy last month was such a success. Did you had traveled there before, or was that your first time to go to Italy?

3.3.30. Find the eight errors with past time in this student writing.

> The event that I will never forget is the day when a snake is really close
>
> to me. I remember that it was a Tuesday because that is the day that
>
> garbage is collected in my neighborhood. I was walking outside with a
>
> big bag of trash and was thinking about all the other things that I had to
>
> do that day. I just set the garbage bag down on the curb when I was hear
>
> an unusual sound. It was a very slow and steady hissing sound. I had
>
> been so nervous. I was confused because I was not know what to do. My
>
> first reaction was to turn and run, but I did not know if making a
>
> sudden movement was a good idea or not. After two or three seconds of
>
> listening to that hissing, I have decided to run away as fast as I could.
>
> When I was about thirty feet away, I looked back. However, by the time I
>
> looked back, the snake already started its escape. I saw the snake writhing
>
> away. I am glad that I was not see the snake when it was near me.

 ## Action Research Project to Inform Your Teaching

Find a transcript of a live conversation. Examine the transcript for all occurrences of past tense verbs. Categorize the tenses. Does any one tense dominate?

ELL Grammar Key 4: *Verb Tenses to Express Future Time* (HB pp. 138–151)

3.4.1. We have a special word *will* just for future tense, but what is ironic about this word?

_____

_____

3.4.2. There are six verb tenses and one special verb expression that express some aspect of future time. Complete this chart with original examples of these verb tenses and verb expressions.

Verb Tense / Expression	Future Meaning	Example
be going to	an event in the future, especially one already planned	
Simple Future Tense	an event in the future, especially one that is scheduled or expresses strong desire to do something	
Present Progressive Tense	an event in the future	
Simple Present Tense	1. a future action marked by a specific future adverb 2. a future action in a dependent clause (no future tense permitted in a dependent clause)	
Future Progressive Tense	an action that will be taking place at some point in the future	
Future Perfect Tense	an action that will be finished by a specified time in the future	
Future Perfect Progressive Tense	how long an action has been happening at a future point; focus is on the duration	

3.4.3. When do we use *be going to* for an action in the future?

_____

_____

_____

3.4.4. How many forms does the verb *take* have with the expression *be going to*? Write them here.

_____

3.4.5. Can you identify and explain these common ELL errors with this grammar point? Match the number of the type of error with its example.

Errors with *be going to*

1. Don't forget to use **be**.
2. Don't forget the word **to**. It's a small but very important word.
3. Don't use **–s** or **–ed** or **–ing** with the verb after **to**.

Student Errors

_____ a. *Why is the bus driver going to stops at every corner?*

_____ b. *On May 17ᵗʰ, the players on this team going to take part in a tournament.*

_____ c. *It's almost noon. If you don't hurry, you going to miss your train to Houston.*

_____ d. *After you take this medicine, I know that you're going feel much better.*

_____ e. *Some of the people at this play are going to attended the play tomorrow night, too.*

3.4.6. What are two uses of *will*?

a. _____

b. _____

3.4.7. How many forms does the verb *take* have with *will*? Write them here.

_____

3.4.8. Can you identify and explain these common ELL errors with this grammar point? Match the number of the type of error with its example.

Errors with *will*

1. Do not use **to** after **will**.
2. Do not add any endings (**–s**, **–ed**, or **–ing**) to verbs after *will*.
3. Use **be going to** (not **will**) to talk about a future event that you have already planned.

Student Errors

_____ a. I have a vacation next week. I will fly to France.

_____ b. When will Flight 662 from New York arrives in Istanbul?

_____ c. Will you to help me with this project? I'm completely lost.

_____ d. Our boss has announced that he and his family will not to attend the party.

_____ e. According to many real estate experts, the housing market will continues to be weak for another two or three years.

_____ f. Jenni just got in her car because she will drive to the bank now.

3.4.9. How many forms does the verb *take* have in the present progressive tense? Write them here.

_____

3.4.10. Can you identify and explain these common ELL errors with this grammar point? Match the number of the type of error with its example.

Errors with Present Progressive Tense for Future Time

1. Don't forget to use **be.**

2. To use present progressive tense for future time, there must be a clear future time established in the conversation, either by the speaker or by the previous speaker.

    unclear: I am leaving for Miami.

    clear: I am leaving for Miami tomorrow.

Student Errors

_____ a. *Paul is grilling some of the steaks that he bought.*

_____ b. *After this class, some of the students meeting to study for the final exam.*

_____ c. *My father-in-law repairing our fence next Saturday if the weather is good.*

_____ d. *We are planning the details of our beach trip.*

3.4.11. The *Keys to Teaching ELL Grammar Handbook* lists two usages for simple present tense to express future time. Fill in this chart with an original example for each usage and the important time words that often accompany each usage.

No.	Usage	Original Example	Key Words
1	with a future time adverb		
2	in a time clause		

3.4.12. In general, we do not use **will** in a time clause. You may, however, see **will** in a dependent clause, but the meaning is different. Give an original example and explain what the **will** means.

_____

_____

3.4.13. Can you identify and explain these common ELL errors with this grammar point? Match the number of the type of error with its example.

Errors with Simple Present Tense for Future Time

1. Do not use simple present tense for a future action without a future time marker.

    unclear: I leave for Miami.

    clear: I leave for Miami around noon tomorrow.

2. Do not use **will** or **be going to** in a future time clause. Use simple present tense.

Student Errors

_____ a. *When we will check out tomorrow, then you and I can split the bill, ok?*

_____ b. *As soon as you will reach Abu Dhabi, will you call me to let me know that you've arrived safely?*

_____ c. *Barb takes her driving test.*

_____ d. *After you are going to finish your work, do you want to have dinner together?*

_____ e. *The weather report says that the good weather continues.*

3.4.14. How many forms does the verb *take* have in future progressive tense? Write them here.

_____

3.4.15. Can you identify and explain these common ELL errors with this grammar point? Match the number of the type of error with its example.

┌───┐
│   │
│   Errors with Future Progressive Tense   │
│   │
│   1. Do not forget to use **be** and a present participle for future progressive tense. │
│   2. Do not use future progressive tense for a short action even though it is happening │
│   in future time.   │
│   *wrong:* If you need help tomorrow, I will be helping you.   │
│   *correct:* If you need help tomorrow, I will help you.   │
│   │
└───┘

Student Errors

_____ a. *At noon tomorrow, we will taking our final exam in this course.*

_____ b. *When I get an email from Jack, I will be reading it immediately.*

_____ c. *If your car won't start, William will be helping you.*

_____ d. *When you arrive at the Cairo airport, I will waiting for you.*

3.4.16. How many forms does the verb *take* have in future perfect tense? Write them here.

_____

3.4.17. Typical ELL Errors

Can you identify and explain these common ELL errors with this grammar point? Match the number of the type of error with its example.

Errors with Future Perfect Tense

1. Do not use future perfect without reference to a second future action or event.

2. Do not use any future tense in a time clause.

Student Errors

_____ a. *We will have finished our exam.*

_____ b. *When she will have finished eating, she will watch her favorite TV show.*

_____ c. *As soon as you will have woken up, please call me.*

_____ d. *Everyone agrees that it is good that the workers will have received a special bonus.*

3.4.18. How many forms does the verb *take* have in future perfect progressive tense? Write them here.

_____

3.4.19. Can you identify and explain these common ELL errors with this grammar point? Match the number of the type of error with its example.

Errors with Future Perfect Progressive Tense

1. In future perfect progressive tense, do not forget to use **has/have been** and the present participle.

2. Do not use future perfect progressive without reference to a second future action or event.

   unclear: We will have been waiting.

   clear: We will have been waiting for three hours by the time your flight arrives.

Student Errors

_____ a. *The clerk will have been standing on her feet for seven consecutive hours.*

_____ b. *I will be living in this same apartment for a full year by the time you graduate.*

_____ c. *This commercial will have been playing on TV for almost six months.*

_____ d. *At the end of this month, I will be working here for five years. I wonder if it's time for a change.*

3.4.20. How do you form the negative of these verb tenses?

Verb Tense/ Expression	Negative Form
be going to	
Present Progressive	
Simple Present	
Simple Future	
Future Progressive	
Future Perfect	
Future Perfect Progressive	

3.4.21. Of the six tenses and one expression for expressing future time, which is the most difficult in your opinion for ELLs to negate? Explain your answer.

_____

_____

_____

3.4.22. Can you identify and explain these common ELL errors with this grammar point? Match the number of the type of error with its example.

Errors with Negating Verbs in Future Time

1. With **be going to,** don't forget to use the correct form of **be.**
2. Do not use **don't, doesn't,** or **didn't** to make negative of **will.**

   wrong: Kathy doesn't will attend the meeting tomorrow.

   correct: Kathy will not attend the meeting tomorrow.

Student Errors

_____ a. *According to the most recent weather report, severe weather not going to hit our area until tomorrow night. Everyone should be prepared for these storms.*

_____ b. *Unfortunately, Joshua's parents do not will attend his graduation ceremony.*

_____ c. *Does your family need a vacation? Surely your family are not going to wait any longer to make plans for your family's fun trip, right?*

_____ d. *I think our professor doesn't will give a quiz tomorrow.*

_____ e. *Now that Ohio has increased the amount of early voting time, voters in that midwestern state not going to experience the long voting lines that they did on the last election day.*

Verb Tense/ Expression	Affirmative	Negative
be going to; Present Progressive		
Simple Future; Future Progressive; Future Perfect; Future Perfect Progressive		
Simple Present		

Verb Tense/ Expression	Question Form
Simple Present	
be going to	
Present Progressive	
Simple Future	
Future Progressive	
Future Perfect	
Future Perfect Progressive	

3.4.23. Complete this chart with the possible contractions.

3.4.24. Complete this chart with the question forms of these verb tenses.

3.4.25. Can you identify and explain these common ELL errors with this grammar point? Match the number of the type of error with its example.

Errors with Forming Questions for Future Time Verbs

1. Do not use **do, does,** or **did** in a question with **will.**

2. Be sure that the subject comes just after the auxiliary verb in questions using **be going to,** present progressive, simple future, future progressive, future perfect, and future perfect progressive.

Student Errors

_____ a. *How many days the teacher will be absent from class?*

_____ b. *Do you will go to the graduation ceremony next week?*

_____ c. *Does the basketball coach will put the player from Serbia in the game tonight?*

_____ d. *When the replacement bridge across the bay will be finished?*

_____ e. *How long the committee is going to meet to discuss the company's problems?*

> Every summer Jim and I take a trip, and this summer is no exception.
>
> In fact, our trip this summer may end up being our best ever because we
>
> go to Italy. We have been looking forward to this trip to Italy for a long
>
> time, and next week we are fly there. Finally, our trip is going to
>
> happening. We have a great guidebook and will continue looking at
>
> information on as many websites as possible right up until the day we will
>
> leave. We don't know many specific details about the places we'll visiting,
>
> but by the time our flight will leave here, we will have reading a lot and
>
> be much better prepared to see Italy. When our flight will take off, I know
>
> that both of us will be so happy that our dream to see Rome and Florence
>
> will finally become a reality.

 3.4.26. Find the eight errors with future time in this student writing.

Action Research Project to Inform Your Teaching

How do spoken language and written language differ on how they treat future verbs? Analyze a transcript of spoken language and an excerpt from a newspaper or website on the same topic. Find out how often any verbs discuss a future action and which verb tenses are used for those discussions. Are they any differences in how future time actions are expressed?

ELL Grammar Key 5: *Count and Non-Count Nouns* (HB pp. 152–160)

3.5.1. What is a count noun? _____

_____

3.5.2. Give 12 examples of count nouns.

_____   _____   _____   _____

_____   _____   _____   _____

_____   _____   _____   _____

Determiner	Determiner + Noun	Determiner + Descriptive Adjective + Noun
articles		
demonstrative		
number		
possessive		
quantifier		

3.5.3. Fill in this chart with appropriate examples.

Sentence 1: For her birthday, Joanna received a watch made in Switzerland.	Sentence 2: For her birthday, Joanna received a designer watch made in Switzerland.

3.5.4. Which of these two sentences is probably more difficult for ELLs to remember to use the indefinite article *a*? _____
Why? _____

_____

3.5.5. Give three examples of idiomatic expressions where singular count nouns are used with no article.

_____   _____   _____

3.5.6. What is a non-count noun?

_____

_____

3.5.7. Give 12 examples of non-count nouns.

_____	_____	_____	_____
_____	_____	_____	_____
_____	_____	_____	_____

3.5.8. Non-count nouns tend to occur in certain categories such as foods. List four other categories, and fill in this chart with two examples for each category.

Category	Examples	
1. *foods*		
2.		
3.		
4.		
5.		

3.5.9. Sometimes we want to quantify a non-count noun. What are three words that we use to quantify non-count nouns?

a. _____   b. _____   c. _____

3.5.10. Give an example of the word *piece* as a quantifier for non-count nouns. Why is this word potentially problematic for ELLs?

_____

_____

_____

3.5.11. In many languages, the question forms *how many* and *how much* are often expressed by the same word. What is the difference in usage between these two phrases in English?

_____

_____

_____

3.5.12. In terms of count and non-count nouns, when do we use the expression *a lot of* in English? What about *a lot?*

_____

_____

_____

_____

3.5.13. The phrases *a few* and *a little* are often expressed by the same word in many languages. What is the difference in usage between these two phrases in English?

_____

_____

3.5.14. Some ELLs confuse the phrase *a little* in these sentences:

     I have a little watch.   vs.   *I have a little time.*

What is the difference in meaning here between *a little* in these two sentences?

_____

_____

_____

3.5.15. Can you explain the difference between *I have a little money* and *I have little money?*

_____

_____

_____

3.5.16. Many ELLs, especially those who are immersed in English classes, overuse the expression *a lot (of)*. While this expression is correct in informal language, what are some words or phrases that all students should use to express this same idea in formal writing or speaking?

_____

_____

3.5.17. Can you identify and explain these common ELL errors with this grammar point? Match the number of the type of error with its example.

Errors with Count/Non-Count Nouns

1. Do not use a singular count noun without an article or other determiner.
2. Non-count nouns do not have a plural form, so do not add **–s**.
3. Do not use **a** or **an** before a non-count noun. With non-count nouns, you cannot use **a** or **an** for the same reason you cannot use one (or two or ten).
4. Avoid using **much** in affirmative statements. It is not necessarily wrong, but it can sound strange in some cases.
5. Do not use **a lot of** without a noun after it. Add a noun or drop the preposition **of**.

Student Errors

_____ a. My area doesn't have a good system of transportation, so it's important to have good car.

_____ b. She's a great teacher. Her students always do their homeworks.

_____ c. The most interesting person in my family is Uncle Tony. He's been plumber all his life.

_____ d. This spicy chicken has chili peppers on it. I like hot peppers, but this dish really has a lot of.

_____ e. Our boss is so good. He just ordered a new equipment to make our job easier.

_____ f. I always ask Aunt Susan whenever I need an important advice.

_____ g. If we don't get there early, there may not be any more bikes on sale. I don't think they have a lot of.

_____ h. She's been studying a lot. She believes she's making a good progress now.

_____ i. Let's walk slowly, ok? We have much time.

_____ j. If I am part-time student, I cannot be considered for any scholarships.

_____ k. In my training course, we have to conduct a research about a certain topic.

_____ l. The seminar leader gave all of the participants a list of ideas for a possible research, and we have to choose one for each of our groups.

3.5.18. Find the eight errors about count and non-count in this student writing.

> Do you have a good credit? Do you remember when you applied for
> your first credit card? Have you ever been declined for credit card from
> company because of your credit history? Well, if you have had that experience,
> you know what a credit card is. According to the <u>msnmoney.com</u> website,
> many American carry between five to ten credit card. Other people carry
> up to 50, which is really a lot of. As we all know, having too much credit
> cards has a negative effect on credit report.

 ## Action Research Project to Inform Your Teaching

Examine the first 250 words of any text written by a native speaker (e.g., from a newspaper or the Internet). Underline all the nouns. How many are count? How many are non-count? Which modifiers are used in front of singular count nouns? Which are used with plural count nouns? Which are used with non-count nouns?

ELL Grammar Key 6: *Prepositions* (HB pp. 161–178)

KEY 6

3.6.1. What is a preposition? _____

_____

3.6.2. Give 12 examples of prepositions.

_____   _____   _____   _____

_____   _____   _____   _____

_____   _____   _____   _____

3.6.3. ELLs may have difficulties with prepositions for the following four reasons. Choose a reason that best describes an error made in each sentence. Use each reason once.

1. Prepositions do not translate well from one language to another.
2. One language requires a preposition after a certain word but another language does not.
3. A language does not have the same word order for prepositions as English does.
4. A preposition used in an idiom is a problem as idioms defy translation.

_____ a. A Spanish speaker said, *"I work in the bank. It's in Green St."*

_____ b. A French speaker wrote, *She is married with John.*

_____ c. *Once at a blue moon, it snows in Florida.*

_____ d. *Let's go bus by.*

_____ e. *They walked the park.*

3.6.4. Give four examples of idioms in English that make use of prepositions. (Do not use the ones given in the *Keys to Teaching ELL Grammar Handbook.*)

_____   _____

_____   _____

3.6.5. What is a prepositional phrase? _____

_____

3.6.6. Decide if each prepositional phrase indicates place, time, or direction, and write it in the corresponding column.

by noon	*in the park*	*to the bus station*
behind the house	*at 3 PM*	*around 7 PM*
from school	*on October 7th*	*next to the tree*
on an island	*toward the light*	*into the forest*

Place	Time	Direction

3.6.7. Label each word in the following prepositional phrases. Some phrases may have only a preposition and an object. Others may also have an article and/or adjective.

Example: in his backyard   **prep + adj + obj**

    a. over the rainbow _____ _____ _____

    b. in January _____ _____

    c. at a great price _____ _____ _____ _____

    d. above all _____ _____

    e. to the train station _____ _____ _____ _____

3.6.8. Give three examples of prepositional phrases, one each with two, three, and four words. Label each part (prep, article, adj, obj).

two words   _____

three words _____

four words   _____

3.6.9. a. When a sentence has both a prepositional phrase of place and of time, which one usually goes first?

_____

Give two examples to illustrate the rule.

_____

_____

b. When there are two prepositional phrases of place and two of time in the same sentence, how should they be arranged?

_____

Give an example of this.

_____

3.6.10. Give eight examples of one-word prepositions.

_____   _____   _____   _____

_____   _____   _____   _____

3.6.11. Give eight examples of two-word prepositions.

_____   _____   _____   _____

_____   _____   _____   _____

3.6.12. Give four examples of three-word prepositions.

_____   _____   _____   _____

3.6.13. How would you explain to an ELL learner the difference in usage of the following prepositions? Provide examples for each use.

	Place	Time
at		
on		
in		

3.6.14. ELLs often confuse the prepositions *for* and *since*. What is the difference in usage between these two prepositions in English? Illustrate with examples.

_____

_____

3.6.15. ELLs often confuse the words *before* and *ago* (for past time). What is the difference in usage between these two words in English? Illustrate with examples.

_____

_____

3.6.16. ELLs often confuse the prepositions *in* and *after* (for future time). What is the difference in usage between these two prepositions in English? Illustrate with examples.

_____

_____

_____

3.6.17. ELLs often confuse the prepositions *for* and *during*. What is the difference in usage between these two prepositions in English? Illustrate with examples.

_____

_____

_____

3.6.18. What should a teacher explain to an ELL who says, "I entered in the house at noon" or "She went the movie last night"?

_____

_____

3.6.19. Which three techniques should ELLs use to learn preposition combinations? Which one of those works well after direction instruction? Why?

_____

_____

3.6.20. Grouping all adjective + preposition combinations by the preposition is one trick to help your ELLs learn the prepositions. Complete the following table using the list of preposition combinations in your textbook. Then do the same with nouns + prepositions and verbs + prepositions. The first adjective set has been done for you.

Preposition Combinations

to	with	of
accustomed to *confusing to* *harmful to* *important to* *married to* *opposed to* *related to* *similar to*		

about	at	for

by	from	in

3.6.21. Look at these idioms with prepositions, and decide how they do or do not contribute toward the overall meaning of the idiom.

Idiom	The Contribution of the Preposition to the Idiom's Meaning
a. *be fed up*	_____
b. *on the dot*	_____
c. *Not on your life!*	_____
d. *over one's head*	_____
e. *under the weather*	_____

3.6.22. Can you identify and explain these common ELL errors with this grammar point? Match the number of the type of error with its example.

Errors with Prepositions

1. Do not forget to use a preposition.
2. Do not use **at** with years or with cities or other large geographical locations.
3. Do not use **in** for streets or days (dates).
4. Do not use **in** with specific names of businesses or the like. Use **at**.
5. Be careful with prepositions for special phrases with *morning, afternoon, evening,* and *night*.

Student Errors

_____ a. *I always eat breakfast at morning.*

_____ b. *She was vacation in California last month.*

_____ c. *The museum is in Blake Street. You can't miss it.*

_____ d. *My mother graduated from college at 1973.*

_____ e. *Yesterday, I had dinner in McDonald's.*

_____ f. *Juan bought Maria a ring in their wedding anniversary.*

_____ g. *Angel Falls, the tallest waterfall, is at Venezuela.*

_____ h. *He does not work in Price Waterhouse anymore.*

_____ i. *Before coming home, he stopped the post office to check his mail box.*

_____ j. *At the afternoon, they went to see a movie.*

_____ k. *We agreed to meet 2 o'clock, but she did not come.*

_____ l. *The tallest building in the world will be built at Dubai.*

3.6.23. Can you identify and explain these common ELL errors with preposition combinations? Match the number of the type of error with its example.

Typical ELL Errors with Preposition Combinations

1. Be sure to use the correct preposition for the word combination that you are using.
2. If you use a verb form after a preposition, it must end in **–ing** (i.e., gerund).
3. With adjectives, one of the most common errors is using the preposition **for** too often.

Student Errors

_____ a. She tried her best, but she was bad in playing golf.

_____ b. He was seriously worried for his sister's health.

_____ c. The student apologized for not come to class on time.

_____ d. Everyone complains about pay such high gas prices.

_____ e. Jane was excited for her sister's wedding.

_____ f. The geography of Chile is not similar with the geography of any other country.

_____ g. Tim looks like Craig, but they are not related for each other.

_____ h. No one was happy for the announcement. It made everyone upset.

_____ i. They dream about to go on vacation next year.

_____ j. He did not have an excuse for not to attend class.

_____ k. My brother is interested about cars. He reads a lot about them and visits car shows all over the state.

_____ l. To my opinion, that was not the best thing to do.

3.6.24. Find eight errors in preposition usage in this student writing.

> *Let me tell you my uncle Luis. He is the most hard-working person I know. He started working at the family farm when he was just twelve years old. Because he worked and took care about the family, he never went in college, but he is smart with life. Everyone in the family has a lot respect to him, and all family members come to him about advice. He is funny and welcoming, but in the same time, he is always willing to help anyone in need.*

Action Research Project to Inform Your Teaching

Ask students of different first languages to translate the following ten sentences into their native language and label each word. Compare the use of prepositions with English. Predict what errors speakers of those languages would be most likely to make with prepositions.

1. My house is in Florida.

2. Las Vegas is in Nevada.

3. The office is on Park Avenue.

4. We went to the beach on Memorial Day.

5. Her sister works at Siemens.

6. I read books in the evening.

7. She is afraid of dogs.

8. Zack talked to his grandmother to get advice on his upcoming marriage.

9. Who is in charge of this project?

10. I agree with you.

ELL Grammar Key 7: *Articles* (HB pp. 179–184)

3.7.1. List two indefinite and one definite article.

Indefinite articles: _____   _____

Definite article: _____

3.7.2. Why does the use of no (zero) article pose a problem for ELLs? _____

_____

3.7.3. Write *a* or *an* in front of the following nouns.

_____ house   _____ university   _____ clock

_____ hour   _____ key   _____ book

_____ uniform   _____ apple   _____ idea

3.7.4. Explain to an ELL the difference in usage between the indefinite articles *a* and *an*. Illustrate the rule with your own examples. Why may words that begin with letters *h* or *u* be problematic?

_____

_____

_____

3.7.5. Write your own sentences and/or phrase to illustrate the use of the definite article *the*. Keep the vocabulary appropriate to the grade/level you will teach/are teaching.

Definite Article: *the*	
Rule	**Example**
1. Use *the* when you are talking about something specific.	
2. Use *the* when the speaker and the listener are talking about the same specific item.	
3. Use *the* for the second and all other references to the same noun.	
4. Use *the* with the superlative form of an adjective, which means with the word *most* or with the ending *–est*.	
5. Use *the* for the names of countries that look plural, including countries that end in *–s* or have the words *united, union, republic,* or *kingdom*.	
6. Use *the* for the parts of something. (Exception: In general, we do not use *the* for body parts.)	
7. Use *the* with most bodies of water except individual lakes.	
8. Use *the* with geographic parts of the globe and geographic areas, deserts, and peninsulas.	

3.7.6. Some ELLs produce sentences such as

    a. The apples are my favorite fruit.
    b. It was obvious that he had the great love for his wife.

What is the problem? As a teacher, explain the issue to the student.

_____

_____

_____

_____

3.7.7. Find an ELL error in each phrase. Correct it. Explain the rule.

a. *a excellent job* _____

b. *a good advice* _____

c. *in United States* _____

d. *most wonderful person* _____

e. *Gulf of Mexico* _____

f. *the honesty* _____

3.7.8. Can you identify and explain these common ELL errors with this grammar point? Match the number of the type of error with its example.

Errors with Articles

1. Do not use a singular count noun without an article (or other determiner).
2. Do not use **a** with a word that begins with a vowel sound or **an** with a word that begins with a consonant sound.
3. Do not use **the** with a plural noun that refers to the whole category.
4. Do not use **the** with abstract nouns or ideas.

Student Errors

_____ a. My cousin showed the courage when he pulled a girl out of a burning house.

_____ b. What great day today was! It was sunny, warm, and relaxing.

_____ c. My father dislikes the lawyers. He says that they are not always honest.

_____ d. I have spent more than a hour waiting for my friend.

_____ e. I respect my best friend because he shows the kindness to all.

_____ f. When we first came to Vermont, we stayed in an hotel.

_____ g. My family bought house in this neighborhood last year. We are very happy with it.

_____ h. In the private school that my brother and I attended, everyone had to wear an uniform.

_____ i. Do you know capital of Venezuela?

_____ j. In general, children do not like the vegetables very much.

_____ k. The intelligence is not the only quality necessary to be admitted to college.

_____ l. The firefighters have a dangerous but extremely important job.

3.7.9. Find eight errors in article usage in this student writing.

I am originally from Sao Paolo. It is the great town with over 15
million people. The people in the Brazil call Sao Paolo financial capital of
the country because a city has lot of banks and businesses. It is like New
York. Living in Sao Paolo may seem difficult to some. A traffic is always
slow, and a pollution there is becoming big problem, but I love my home
town.

⌕ Action Research Project to Inform Your Teaching

Ask students of different first languages to translate the following sentences into their native language.

1. I have a brother. He is the best brother in the world.

2. Politicians in many countries are corrupt.

3. My sister wants to move to a city in the United States; however, she spent all her life in a village in Colombia.

4. I don't like cookies or chocolate. I prefer things that are not sweet.

5. If you buy a car, you need to take care of it.

Ask them to indicate the article (if any) or explain what happens to the article in their translations. Compare the target language to English. Predict the types of errors in English article usage based on your findings.

ELL Grammar Key 8: *Pronunciation of* –s *and* –ed (HB pp. 185–192)

3.8.1. Which three sounds does a final –*s* make in English when added to a noun or a verb?

_____   _____   _____

3.8.2. Which three sounds does an –*ed* ending make in English when added to a verb?

_____   _____   _____

3.8.3. Why is it so important for ELLs to know the correct pronunciation of –*ed* ending? In how many verb tenses is this ending used?

_____

_____

3.8.4. What does the pronunciation of –*s* or –*ed* depend on?

   a. variations within regional dialects

   b. individual factors such as age, gender, etc.

   c. the final sound of the word before the marker is added

   d. the way the word is currently spelled

3.8.5. What three processes influence the formation of a sound in English?

_____   _____   _____

3.8.6. Can you explain the difference between voiced and voiceless sounds?

_____

_____

3.8.7. The sound /p/ is voiceless, but /b/ is voiced. Decide if the following sounds are voiced or voiceless, and write them in the correct box.

/d/   /g/   /f/   /l/   /o/   /s/   /n/   /θ/   /i/

/k/   /v/   /t/   /m/   /ı/   /r/   /z/   /a/   /ə/

Voiced	Voiceless

3.8.8. Consider the following groups of verbs. Indicate the verb that has a different final sound from the other three. What is its final sound? Then indicate the final sound of the other three verbs.

Verbs	Odd Verb and Its Final Sound	Final Sound of Group of Three Verbs
a. liked, decided, washed, reached		
b. proceeded, followed, planted, accepted		
c. smiled, played, arrived, talked		
d. annoyed, buzzed, bored, blinked		
e. backed, charged, clapped, dressed		

3.8.9. Consider the following groups of nouns. Indicate the odd plural noun that has a different final sound from the other three. What is its final sound? Then indicate the final sound of the other three nouns.

Nouns	Odd Noun and Its Final Sound	Final Sound of Group of Three Nouns
a. pants, tricks, passengers, lamps		
b. monkeys, reasons, shoes, cups		
c. glasses, ties, watches, businesses		
d. walls, faxes, curtains, blinds		
e. toys, carpets, books, pots		

3.8.10. Find all words that end with the letter –*s*. Decide if each word is a verb (V) or a noun (N) and if it makes /s/, /z/, or /əz/ sound. Follow the example.

Example: He think**s (V, /s/)** that his new shoe**s (N, /z/)** do not fit him well.

a. Maria enjoys reading books and listening to operas.

b. Sam takes the subway to school every day. He never arrives late.

c. Anne wears glasses to avoid wearing contacts.

d. I love fresh snacks. My favorites are apples, pears, apricots, and bananas.

e. John likes vegetables. He cannot live without tomatoes, cucumbers, radishes, and potatoes.

3.8.11. Can you explain the pronunciation rules for –*s* ending?

_____

_____

_____

3.8.12. Can you explain the pronunciation rules for –*ed* ending?

_____

_____

_____

3.8.13. Place these verbs into the respective columns by their final sound.

avoided	calculated	faxed	guided
disarmed	educated	extended	guarded
chewed	closed	fetched	influenced
disliked	faced	explained	imagined

/t/	/d/	/əd/

3.8.14. Place the following words into the respective columns by their final sound.

cats	plants	judges	works
bees	dogs	trees	reaches
birds	houses	elephants	washes
dresses	giraffes	arrives	follows

/s/	/z/	/əz/

3.8.15. To make it easier for the students to hear the final sound, put each given word in a phrase or a sentence in which the next word begins with a vowel sound.

breaks _____

liked _____

raised _____

plays _____

3.8.16. Your ELL student says *frogs, zebras,* and *lions* with final /s/ instead of /z/. How would you help the student?

_____

_____

_____

3.8.17. Give eight original examples of verbs that end with –*ed* that end in the sound /t/.

_____   _____   _____   _____

_____   _____   _____   _____

3.8.18. Give eight original examples of verbs that end with –*ed* that end in the sound /d/.

_____   _____   _____   _____

_____   _____   _____   _____

3.8.19. Give eight original examples of verbs that end with –*ed* that end in the sound /əd/.

_____   _____   _____   _____

_____   _____   _____   _____

3.8.20. Give eight original examples of words that end with –*s* that end in the sound /s/.

_____   _____   _____   _____

_____   _____   _____   _____

3.8.21. Give eight original examples of words that end with –*s* that end in the sound /z/.

_____   _____   _____   _____

_____   _____   _____   _____

3.8.22. Give eight original examples of words that end with –*s* that end in the sound /əz/.

_____   _____   _____   _____

_____   _____   _____   _____

3.8.23. Circle the ten common ELL errors with –s /–ed endings and explain them. Each sentence has at least one error.

a. She comes (come + /s/) to class on time unlike some of the other students (student + /s/).

_____

b. Sharon never gives (give + /s/) up. She perseveres (persevere + /s/) and then celebrates (celebrate + /s/) her victories (victory + /z/).

_____

c. Dan has a lot of books (book + /s/). He needs (need + /s/) to buy at least two cabinets (cabinet + /s/) to arrange all the volumes (volume + /s/).

_____

d. My grandmother often joked (joke + /t/) that she never measured (measure + /t/) anything when she cooked (cook + /əd/) even when she baked (bake + /t/) her famous pies.

_____

e. Alan mixed (mix + /əd/) up the keys (key + /s/) and could not enter the apartment he moved (move + /d/) into last week.

_____

f. As soon as she invited (invite + /əd/) us for dinner, our conversation was interrupted (interrupt + /əd/) by a bunch of screaming kids (kid + /s/).

_____

3.8.24. Find eight errors in –*s* / –*ed* pronunciation.

Karen:	Hi, Jim. How are you today? I heard you have a big engineering exam coming soon.
Jim:	Gosh, don't remind me about it. I have been studying for it every night after work for three months (month + /z/) now. I am sick of it.
Karen:	Ah! You have been studying. I doubted (doubt + /əd/) you would do the same thing you did last time.
Jim:	Man! Never again. I waited (wait + /əd/) until two weeks (week + /z/) before the exam and then started (start + /əd/) studying. I failed (fail + /t/) it by two points (point + /z/).
Karen:	Ouch! That must have made you mad.
Jim:	Mad? Are you kidding? I was furious. The worst thing was my mother's (mother + /s/) reaction, "Uhm, I told you to take it more seriously." Does (do + /s/) she have to be right about everything?
Karen:	She only wants (want + /s/) what's (what + /z/) best for you. When is the exam?
Jim:	In two days (day + /s/).
Karen:	Wow, so soon. You'd better get back to your books (book + /s/).
Jim:	Great! You too. I have done enough studying. I need a break.
Karen:	You will have lots (lot + /s/) of time to rest after the exam.
Jim:	Ha, easy for you to say.
Karen:	Good luck! You will need it.

⊘ *Action Research Project to Inform Your Teaching*

What is the most common way to make nouns plural in English? Make a list of 25 animal names at random. Eliminate any animals that have irregular plurals (*deer* → *deer* or *mouse* → *mice*). After you have your list of words, determine the percentage of your words that end in /s/, /z/, and /əz/. (HINT: If you get stuck, pretend you are walking through a zoo.)

ELL Grammar Key 9: *Adjective Clauses and Reductions* (HB pp. 193–200)

3.9.1. What is an adjective clause?

_____

_____

3.9.2. What is a typical position of an adjective clause in an English sentence?

_____

3.9.3. List relative pronouns that begin adjective clauses in English. Which ones of them may be omitted and when?

_____

_____

3.9.4. In English, which relative pronouns are used for people and which ones for things? Are there any that can be used for both?

_____

_____

3.9.5. Write three sentences where a relative pronoun is a subject in an adjective clause.

a. _____

b. _____

c. _____

3.9.6. Write three sentences where a relative pronoun is an object in an adjective clause.

a. _____

b. _____

c. _____

3.9.7. To ensure the understanding of adjective clauses by ELLs, which type of adjective clauses (clauses in which the relative pronoun functions as the subject or clauses in which the relative pronoun functions as an object) should be taught first and why?

_____

_____

3.9.8. What is a reduced adjective clause?

_____

_____

3.9.9. Write four sentences containing reduced adjective clauses.

a. _____

b. _____

c. _____

d. _____

3.9.10. When an adjective clause has *who/which/that* as the subject and any form of *be*, what needs to be done to reduce the clause? Illustrate the rule with your own examples.

_____

_____

_____

_____

3.9.11. When an adjective clause has *who/which/that* as the subject followed by a verb, what needs to be done to reduce the clause? Illustrate the rule with your own examples.

_____

_____

_____

_____

3.9.12. Can you identify and explain these common ELL errors with this grammar point? Match the number of the type of error with its example.

Errors with Adjective Clauses and Reductions

1. Do not forget to use a relative pronoun (**who, that, which**).
2. Do not use the wrong word to begin a relative clause. Do not use **which** for people or **who** for things in relative clauses.
3. Do not include an unnecessary (extra) pronoun in a relative clause.
4. Don't forget to omit both the subject and the verb **be**. You can't omit just one of them.

Student Errors

_____ a. *The house which we saw it last week was taken off the market.*

_____ b. *The house is at 1672 Fifth Street needs a new roof.*

_____ c. *The Eiffel Tower, which built in 1889, has been visited by more than 200 million people.*

_____ d. *The salesclerk which helped me find pine nuts was very patient.*

_____ e. *The woman gave me flowers was very nice.*

_____ f. *The dancer that I told you about her is coming to town.*

_____ g. *The boat who was on sale was sold in less than a week.*

_____ h. *The last book that written by J.K. Rowling sold millions.*

_____ i. *I was lucky to help the man who writing a screen play that later turned into a blockbuster.*

_____ j. *I have never met anyone is more dedicated than my sister.*

_____ k. *The shoes that she picked them were not her size.*

_____ l. *The neighbor's car who is parked outside of our house damages our grass.*

3.9.13. Find eight errors in adjective clause and reductions usage in this student writing.

> My family lives in an apartment is not very big. The building which the apartment is located in has nine floors, and our apartment is on the eighth floor. It has three bedrooms, a kitchen, and a bathroom. The room who my sister and I share is smaller than the other two rooms. Our room has a bunk bed saves a lot of space. Our parents have their own room is right next to ours. Down the corridor, we have a living room also serves as our dining room because it is located very close to the kitchen. The kitchen that my mom cooks every day has a lot of plants. The apartment that live in is nice, but I wish it were a bit bigger. The room where sleep my sister and I is too small.

 Action Research Project to Inform Your Teaching

Examine a content book (e.g., a science book or a business website) written by native speakers. Identify all adjective clauses (both full and reduced forms). For those that describe a person, how many use *who/whom* and how many use *that*? What percentage of clauses are full and what percentage are reduced?

ELL Grammar Key 10: *Infinitives and Gerunds* (HB pp. 201–209)

3.10.1. What is an infinitive? How does it function in an English sentence?

_____

_____

3.10.2. Give eight examples of infinitives.

_____   _____   _____   _____

_____   _____   _____   _____

3.10.3. What is a gerund? How does it function in an English sentence?

_____

_____

3.10.4. Give eight examples of gerunds.

_____   _____   _____   _____

_____   _____   _____   _____

3.10.5. Write five sentences using gerunds as subjects in your sentences.

a. _____

b. _____

c. _____

d. _____

e. _____

3.10.6. In the following example, what do ELLs need to know about the infinitive and the comma?

Example: To help her mother prepare for the party, Jane left work early on Friday.

_____

_____

3.10.7. What determines whether an infinitive or a gerund needs to be used after a verb? How should ELLs approach gerunds and infinitives?

_____

_____

3.10.8. Arrange the following verbs into the three columns.

intend	be tired of	begin	want
dislike	hate	consider	think about
hesitate	postpone	ask	start

Followed by Infinitives	Followed by Gerunds	Followed by Both

3.10.9. There are a few verbs that can be followed by either an infinitive or a gerund, but the meaning is different. This group includes *remember, stop, try, forget,* and *regret.* Write your own sentences to illustrate the difference.

	VERB + Infinitive	VERB + Gerund
remember		
stop		
try		
forget		
regret		

3.10.10. When an ELL says, *"I need that you help me"* instead of *"I need you to help me,"* what needs to be explained?

_____

_____

_____

3.10.11. Write five sentences using the verbs in the structure: verb + noun/pronoun + infinitive. Label each part of the structure in your examples.

advise	cause	forbid	invite	permit	teach	want
allow	convince	force	need	persuade	tell	warn
ask	expect	get	order	remind	urge	would like

a. _____

b. _____

c. _____

d. _____

e. _____

3.10.12. What makes the verbs *make, let, have* and *help* different?

_____

_____

3.10.13. Preposition + gerund is a very common structure in English. Write four short sentences to illustrate this structure.

a. _____

b. _____

c. _____

d. _____

3.10.14. Can you identify and explain these common ELL errors with this grammar point? Match the number of the type of error with its example.

> ## Errors with Infinitives and Gerunds
>
> 1. Do not use infinitives after verbs that take gerunds (and vice versa).
> 2. The most common verb form for the subject of a sentence is a gerund.
> 3. Don't use a plural verb form with a gerund. Don't be tricked by a plural object after the gerund. The object of a gerund does not affect the verb.

Student Errors

_____ a. *Driving large cars and trucks are not beneficial for the environment.*

_____ b. *I practiced to play the piano so I could perform at the school graduation.*

_____ c. *To give a public speech is something that I have always dreaded.*

_____ d. *Spending money on designer clothes, diamonds, and extravagant vacations are something that very few people in the world can afford.*

_____ e. *Even though I need to drive more to get to my new job, I expect making a lot of money there.*

_____ f. *Ann bought her first book on tape. To listen to books should improve her English.*

_____ g. *My mother and I discussed to go on a trip next spring.*

_____ h. *Recycling newspapers, bottles, and cars are what everyone should do.*

_____ i. *In Japan, to slurp loudly while drinking soup out of a bowl is not considered impolite.*

_____ j. *Since she was a little girl, to attend special classes to learn dance steps from around the world has been my sister's biggest dream.*

_____ k. *Booking flights and vacation packages online rather than through travel agents have proven to be cheaper.*

_____ l. *We decided watching a movie at 6:30 instead of 8 PM because the movie is so long.*

3.10.15. Find eight errors in the infinitive and gerunds usage in this student writing.

> To play in a casino is a kind of entertainment. There are lots of games
>
> choose and play. When you win, you want to come back playing again
>
> and again. It is not even easy for highly paid professionals getting that
>
> kind of money to waste on to gamble. People want to gamble to getting
>
> high returns. However, this may be the beginning of an addiction. Many
>
> people become gamblers because they like to take risks, and they think that
>
> to gamble is a quick and easy way to getting lots of money in a short time.
>
> It is very easy to gamble because there are a lot of casinos where people
>
> can play any time they want.

 ## *Action Research Project to Inform Your Teaching*

How common are infinitves and gerunds in spoken language? Analyze a transcript of spoken language for the number of infinitives and gerunds that are actually used. Are there any patterns that you see emerging?

ELL Grammar Key 11: *Phrasal Verbs* (HB pp. 210–223)

KEY 11

3.11.1. What is a phrasal verb?

_____

_____

3.11.2. Give 12 examples of phrasal verbs.

_____	_____	_____	_____
_____	_____	_____	_____
_____	_____	_____	_____

3.11.3. Look at the following sentences. Decide which ones use phrasal verbs and which ones have a verb + prepositional phrase.

____a. He came up with the money.   ____ d. He came up the ladder.

____b. The car went off the road.   ____ e. The bomb went off at noon.

____c. They looked into the cave.   ____ f. They looked into the problem.

3.11.4. Why do ELLs have difficulties with phrasal verbs?

_____

_____

3.11.5. Why are phrasal verbs so important?

_____

_____

3.11.6. Why do some ELLs, speakers of Latin-based languages in particular, prefer single-word equivalents to phrasal verbs?

_____

_____

3.11.7. Write a phrasal verb that has the same meaning as its single-word equivalent.

a. cancel _____   e. meet_____   i. visit _____

b. solve _____   f. withstand_____   j. continue _____

c. explode _____   g. raise_____   k. increase_____

d. discover _____   h. escape_____   l. enter_____

3.11.8. What is a separable phrasal verb?

_____

_____

3.11.9. Write three sentences with separable phrasal verbs. Use three patterns in each case.

Verb + Noun	Separated by Noun	Separated by Pronoun
1.		
2.		
3.		

3.11.10. What is a non-separable phrasal verb?

_____

_____

3.11.11. Write three sentences with non-separable phrasal verbs. Use two patterns in each case.

Verb + Noun	Verb + Pronoun
1.	
2.	
3.	

3.11.12. Phrasal verbs are usually idiomatic and often have multiple meanings. Think of at least three meanings for each phrasal verb below. Follow the example.

Phrasal Verb	Meaning 1	Meaning 2	Meaning 3
a. *pick up*	*raise*	*increase speed*	*learn without effort*
b. *get through*			
c. *make out*			
d. *make up*			

3.11.13. In order to help ELLs remember multiple meanings of the same phrasal verb, the teacher should have relevant examples. Look at the previous exercise and create sentences or a context explaining multiple meanings of each phrasal verb, including the one used as an example.

Phrasal Verb	Sentence/Context 1	Sentence/Context 2	Sentence/Context 3
a. *pick up*			
b. *get through*			
c. *make out*			
d. *make up*			

3.11.14. What happens when a phrasal verb is intransitive? Give three examples of intransitive phrasal verbs.

_____

_____

3.11.15. Use each intransitive phrasal verb in a sentence.

a. *catch on* _____

b. *grow up* _____

c. *hold on* _____

d. *slow down* _____

e. *take off* _____

3.11.16. Can you identify and explain these common ELL errors with this grammar point? Match the number of the type of error with its example.

Errors with Phrasal Verbs

1. Use phrasal verbs. The single-word alternatives found in a dictionary often sound more technical or formal than the equivalent phrasal verb.
2. Do not confuse the meanings of phrasal verbs.
3. Do not forget to use the whole phrasal verb, not just the verb.
4. Do not forget to separate separable phrasal verbs when there is a pronoun object.

Student Errors

_____ a. The little girl yelled, "Let me exit this taxi now!"

_____ b. On weekends, I do not need to wake early, so I never set my alarm.

_____ c. After a long night of reading and studying for my final exams, I was so tired that I passed away on the couch.

_____ d. Can you help me ascertain the phone number for the post office?

_____ e. Are you taking all the information you need for that test?

_____ f. Will the boss pick down our reports tomorrow?

_____ g. My uncle was coming into town. My mother went to pick up him at the airport.

_____ h. The business proposal is interesting, and I need one night to think it.

_____ i. Teenagers are used to loud music, so my teenager always asks, "Mom, can you please increase the volume of the TV?"

_____ j. The vice president's flight was delayed, so our meeting could not take place. We had to call off it.

_____ k. If he had stopped at a gas station, he would not have run away of gas.

_____ l. Juan is an excellent student. Last week he was one of the few students who turned in his essay on time. This week he turned in it three days early.

3.11.17. Find eight errors in the phrasal verb usage in this student writing.

> Registering for TOEFL (Test of English as a Foreign Language) is a relatively easy thing to do. First, you need to figure which type of TOEFL test to register for. If you want to sign in for the one offered at your school, then you will most likely be studying for a paper-based test. An Internet-based test (iBT) is offered in testing centers around the world, and you must come out with the fee to pay for it. To register for an iBT, you must fill and mail out a form from the TOEFL Bulletin, call at the testing company, or go online. Once you have made your mind up about the test type, calm and try to carefully prepare for it. If you fail, don't be afraid to do over it. You are not alone.

 Action Research Project to Inform Your Teaching

Examine the first 500 words of any text written by a native speaker (e.g., from a newspaper or the Internet). Underline all phrasal verbs. Predict which ones are problematic to ELLs and which ones are not? Explain your predictions.

ELL Grammar Key 12: *Modals* (HB pp. 224–231)

3.12.1. What is a modal verb?

_____

_____

3.12.2. Give eight examples of modal verbs.

_____   _____   _____   _____

_____   _____   _____   _____

3.12.3. Give two reasons why modals are difficult for ELLs as vocabulary words?

_____

_____

3.12.4. Give three reasons why modals are difficult for ELLs grammatically?

_____

_____

_____

3.12.5. What is one of the disadvantages of presenting modals one by one?

_____

3.12.6. What is the reasoning for teaching modals one by one to lower-proficiency students and grouping modals by meaning for higher-proficiency students? What is your opinion?

_____

_____

_____

_____

_____

3.12.7. The modal verb *could* has five meanings, whereas the modal verb *would* has three. Write your own sentences to illustrate each meaning.

could

a. _____

b. _____

c. _____

d. _____

e. _____

would

a. _____

b. _____

c. _____

3.12.8. Write your own sentences to illustrate the use of various modal verbs in the meanings of *request, permission,* and *possibility.*

Modals and Multiple Meanings		
Meanings	**Modals**	**Examples**
Request	*can*	
	could	
	would	
	may	
	might	
Permission	*can*	
	could	
	would	
	may	
Possibility	*may, might, could*	
	should, ought to	
	must	
	will	

3.12.9. Can you identify and explain these common ELL errors with this grammar point? Match the number of the type of error with its example.

Errors with Modals

1. Do not use **to** after single-word modals.

2. Do not add any endings (**–s, –ed,** or **–ing**) to verbs after modals.

3. Do not use **don't, doesn't,** or **didn't** to make negative forms of most modals. Remember that most modals form the negative by adding **not** after the modal. (This is just like with **be** and other auxiliary verbs.)

4. Do not use **do, does,** or **did** in a question with a modal. Most modals form the question by inverting the subject and the modal. (This is just like with **be** and other auxiliary verbs.)

5. Do not use **could** for past ability if it is a single past action in an affirmative sentence. In this case, we use **was able to** or **were able to**. In a negative sentence, **couldn't** and **wasn't able to** or **weren't able to** are okay. We only use **could** for the past of **can** when the action was over a period of time.

Student Errors

_____ a. The tickets were very expensive, so my mother could not attended my graduation.

_____ b. I knew that we could to make it on time if we took the 8:00 train.

_____ c. Does he can help me study for the test? He knows so much.

_____ d. My friend Alan will assists me in moving from my old apartment into a house.

_____ e. My friend doesn't should be so angry all the time.

_____ f. I could finally speak to him on the phone last night after leaving him three messages.

_____ g. Did they could get to see "Indiana Jones" on the opening night?

_____ h. She could buy all her office needs yesterday.

_____ i. The officer told me that I must to show him my driver's license, insurance, and registration.

_____ j. You should driving slowly because of all the traffic.

_____ k. The teacher told us that we might to have a test tomorrow.

_____ l. My aunt didn't could tell me that my grandfather died, so I did not know.

3.12.10. Find eight errors in modals in this student writing.

> *My father always tells me that I will achieving great things if I study hard. I know that he must to be right, but I am not sure what I want to do in life. I liked to build things when I was little, so engineering could becomes my career. My dad is an engineer. He can always helps and guide me when I need his support. On the other hand, I might to consider a career in accounting since I am good with money and finances. It would to be convenient to go to school because one of the best business colleges in the state is next to my house. I am still not sure. I should to think more about it, but one thing is for certain. I can doing anything I want. This is great.*

 ### Action Research Project to Inform Your Teaching

How common are modals? Many people mistakenly believe that modals are relatively rare and are used for only certain kinds of writing. Look up the entry for any animal in an encyclopedia (an online version is good). How many and which modals do you find? What are the meanings of the modals that you find? Before you consult the encyclopedia article, make a ranked list of which modals and meanings you expect to find. Compare your predictions with your actual tallies.

ELL Grammar Key 13: *Word Forms* (HB pp. 232–241)

KEY 13

3.13.1. State the two-step approach to ELLs' learning of word forms. Illustrate with your own examples.

_____

_____

_____

_____

3.13.2. Complete the chart with other possible word forms

	analyze (V)	interpret (V)	respond (V)	create (V)
noun / product	analysis			
noun / person	analyst			
adjective	analytic			
adjective	analytical			
participial adjectives	analyzing analyzed			
adverb	analytically			

3.13.3. Complete the following chart. Underline all suffixes.

Verb	Adjective	Adverb	Noun
	vari*able*		
conceptual*ize*			
		institution*ally*	
	secure		
exclude			

3.13.4. Complete the chart with your own examples of verbs. Give five examples of each type of verb.

Word Endings for Verbs		
Ending	**Meaning**	**Example**
–ate	to cause, to become, to supply with	
–en	to make something have a certain quality	
–ify	to cause or make into something	
–ize	to become	

3.13.5. Complete the chart with two original examples for the selected adjective meanings. Give five examples of each.

Some Word Endings for Adjectives		
Ending	**Meaning**	**Example**
–able, –ible	having a particular quality	
–al	of or relating to something	
–ant, –ent	having the quality of	
–ary	belonging to	
–ative, –itive	having the quality of	
–en	made of	
–ive	having a particular quality	
–less	without something	
–like	similar to	
–ly	having qualities of	
–ory	relating to	
–ous, –ious	having qualities of	
–y	having the character of	

3.13.6. Complete the chart with three original examples of adverbs ending in *–ly.*

Word Ending for Adverbs		
Ending	**Meaning**	**Example**
–ly	in a particular way or at times	

3.13.7. Give six examples of adverbs that do not end in *–ly.*

_____   _____   _____

_____   _____   _____

3.13.8. Give three examples of words that end in *–ly* but are not adverbs.

_____   _____   _____

3.13.9. Complete the chart with three original examples for the selected noun meanings.

Selected Word Endings for Nouns		
Ending	**Meaning**	**Example**
–al	the act of doing something	
–(e)/(a)nce, –cy	action or process; quality	
–er, –or, –ar, –r	someone or something that does something	
–ity, –ty	having a quality	
–tion, –ion	act or result of doing something	
–ism	a belief or set of ideas	
–ment	a result of doing something	
–ness	state or condition	
–ure	an act or process	

3.13.10. Give two original examples of words that can be a noun, a verb, and an adjective without any change in endings. Write sentences with those words to illustrate the meaning. Follow the example of the word *survey*.

	Noun	**Verb**	**Adjective**
survey	She completed a survey.	Every year city officials survey land to be sold.	There were 10 survey questions.

3.13.11. Can you identify and explain these common ELL errors with this grammar point? Match the number of the type of error with its example.

Errors with Word Forms

1. Creating new words with word endings is very difficult. Check a dictionary when you are trying to create a new word.
2. Some adjectives end in –**ly**. (examples: *early, daily, oily, lonely, friendly*)
3. Not all adverbs end in –**ly**. (examples: *fast, well, soon, always, here, hard*)

Student Errors

_____ a. In the writing class, we work a lot on error correctivness.

_____ b. Ella is a very friend person. She has a lot of friends in many countries.

_____ c. If you try hardly, you will be able to pass the test.

_____ d. If he runs fastly, he will be able to beat the Olympic record.

_____ e. My younger brother repeatings everything my older brother does. It is annoying.

_____ f. Even my small hometown used to have a day newspaper.

_____ g. Tom is a very lone person.

_____ h. Everyone loves to hear her wonderness voice.

_____ i. His argumentings are never valid, so one pays much attention to what he says.

_____ j. I am really upset because of the disagree between my sister and me.

_____ k. Janet and Andy bought a new house. They will be moving soonly.

_____ l. The sandwich that I had for lunch yesterday was so oil that I got sick.

3.13.12. Find eight errors in word forms in this student writing.

> *Grammar class is my favorite of all the classes I am taking this semester. There are only fifteen students in this class, and they come from six differently countries. Naturalistically, we all have to speak English. The teacher is so friend. She explanates everything very well and always gives us the answerings to the homework exercises. At the begin of the semester, we received a detailing schedule, so now we know when we have tests and quizzes and when homework assignatures are due. I am learning a lot in this class. I wish I could take more classes with the same teacher next semester.*

 ## Action Research Project to Inform Your Teaching

How good are ELLs at knowing the correct word forms of words in English? Prepare a quiz for an ELL by providing a list of words and then asking the ELL to change the part of speech. For example: *What is the adjective for the noun* color? Prepare ten questions. Before you give your questions to five ELLs to complete, predict which three you think will be the most difficult and which three will be the easiest.

ELL Grammar Key 14: *Passive Voice* (HB pp. 242–251)

3.14.1. Change the following sentences from active to passive voice. Underline the verb.

Active	Passive
Mary wrote six detailed emails.	Six detailed emails <u>were written</u> by Mary.
Children have read this book for almost a century.	
The price of oil will affect our economy for the next decade.	
Three companies are building an arena.	
A tornado destroyed the village.	

3.14.2. Fill in the blanks. The passive voice requires two parts: _____

and _____ .

3.14.3. Change the following sentences from active to passive voice. Keep the same verb tenses. Underline the verb.

Active Voice	Passive Voice
Jane eats an apple every day.	
Jane is eating an apple now.	
Jane has already eaten an apple.	
Jane is going to eat an apple soon.	
Jane had eaten an apple before work.	

3.14.4. Change the following sentences from passive to active voice. Keep the same verb tenses.

Active Voice	Passive Voice
	The car is driven by Bill.
	The car is being driven by Bill.
	The car has been driven by Bill.
	The car was driven by Bill.
	The car was being driven by Bill.
	The car had been driven by Bill.
	The car will be driven by Bill.
	The car will have been driven by Bill.

3.14.5. What makes **active voice** different from **passive voice**?

_____

_____

3.14.6. Write three sentences in **active voice.** Follow Subject + Verb + Object pattern. Label all three parts. Remember that in active voice, the emphasis is always on the subject.

a. _____

b. _____

c. _____

3.14.7. Use the three sentences that you have written for the previous exercise. Change them into **passive voice.** Remember that in passive voice, the subject is the person or thing that "receives" the action of the verb.

a. _____

b. _____

c. _____

3.14.8. Complete the following chart with your own sentences in both **active** and **passive voice.** Underline the predicates in each sentence.

Verb Tense/ Expression	Active Voice Verb	Passive Voice *Be* + Past Participle
Present		
Past		
Present Progressive		
be going to		
Present Perfect		
Modals		

3.14.9. What is an intransitive verb?

_____

_____

3.14.10. Give eight examples of intransitive verbs.

_____   _____   _____   _____

_____   _____   _____   _____

3.14.11. When is passive voice used?

_____

_____

3.14.12. When should the _by_ + doer phrase be used?

_____

_____

3.14.13. Explain to an ELL a difference between _He is married_ and _He got married_. When is _get_ + past participle used in English?

_____

_____

3.14.14. Write three sentences where past participle is used as an adjective and shows state rather than action.

Example: The door is locked.

a. _____

b. _____

c. _____

3.14.15. Some ELLs may have a difficult time understanding and correctly using the following sentences:

    a. I am interested in this class.   b. This class is interesting.

Why? _____

_____

3.14.16. When should ELLs use **present** and when **past participles** as adjectives? Explain the rule.

_____

_____

_____

_____

3.14.17. Use each of the following participles and adjectives in a sentence to illustrate the difference in meaning.

confusing	confused
exciting	excited
puzzling	puzzled

3.14.18. To help ELLs remember **past participle** + **preposition** combinations, group the following phrases by preposition.

be accustomed to	be dedicated to	be finished with	be satisfied with
be acquainted with	be devoted to	be fed up with	be scared of
be ashamed of	be disappointed in/with	be impressed by/with	be surprised at/by
be bored with/by	be divorced from	be interested in	be terrified of
be committed to	be done with	be made of/from	be tired of
be composed of	be dressed in	be married to	be tired from
be confused about	be excited about	be opposed to	be used to
be convinced of	be exhausted from	be related to	be worried about

to	with	of	by

about	from	in	at

3.14.19. Can you identify and explain these common ELL errors with this grammar point? Match the number of the type of error with its example.

Errors with Passive Voice

1. Do not use active voice when you should use passive voice.
2. Do not forget to use a form of **be** in the passive voice.
3. Do not use the **by** + doer phrase if the information is not new or important.
4. Do not mix up when to use **–ing** (present participle) and when to use **–ed** (past participle). They are completely different.
5. Do not forget to use an appropriate ending. Do not use just the simple verb form as an adjective.

Student Errors

_____ a. The car drove by John because he was the only one who knew how to drive a stick shift car.

_____ b. The book which written by that author is now a best seller.

_____ c. The scare child ran to his mother.

_____ d. I collect watches. This one was made in Switzerland by the watch factory workers.

_____ e. The story I started reading was not interested, so I picked another book.

_____ f. The pedestrian who hit the bus was taken to the hospital. He had serious injuries.

_____ g. Seeing Pavarotti perform on stage was an immensely gratify experience.

_____ h. Susan did not know if she was accepted to college or not because her acceptance letter lost in the mail.

_____ i. In computer adaptive testing, the examination questions chose by a special computer program.

_____ j. Spanish is spoken by people in most countries in South American.

_____ k. The President elected by a majority because more than two-thirds of the country voted for him.

_____ l. I was confusing by all of the admission requirements to college.

3.14.20. Find eight errors in passive voice in this student writing.

> When I was worked as an engineer in Cali, Colombia, my company
>
> awarded a multi-million dollar contract to build a new school. The
>
> project was closely supervising by the city officials, and tight deadlines set.
>
> Therefore, we had to work quickly and efficiently. I was assigning as a
>
> project manager and giving tasks that required me to be on site. The
>
> construction was be complicated by constant rains. However, we managed
>
> to complete the school by the next academic year, and the company
>
> chosen as one of the best engineering and construction companies in the
>
> country.

 ## *Action Research Project to Inform Your Teaching*

Give ELLs a list of five participle pairs such as *interested—interesting* or *annoyed—annoying*. Ask ELLs to explain the difference in the pairs and then write examples for both words.

ELL Grammar Key 15: *Conditionals (If Clauses) and* Wish (HB pp. 252–262)

3.15.1. Look at each sentence. Which one refers to present and which one to the past? Why is the same form *took* used in both cases? Which sentence would be hard for ELLs to understand and why?

    a. She *took* the test and passed it.   b. If she *took* the test, she would pass it.

_____

_____

_____

3.15.2. Why would the sentence *If I'd known you were still in town, I would've stopped by,* be difficult for ELLs?

_____

_____

3.15.3. What is a conditional sentence?

_____

_____

3.15.4. Write three sentences with conditional clauses. Make sure that each sentence has a result clause to avoid fragments.

	Result	Conditional
1		
2		
3		

3.15.5. What is the correct way to punctuate conditional sentences?

_____

3.15.6. In actual communication, the *if* clause is often understood or implied and not stated. Write three such sentences. Example: *They surely would have passed the exam.*

a. _____

b. _____

c. _____

3.15.7. Write four sentences (two about the present and two about the past) sentences with *zero conditionals*. Remember that they are used for facts and situations that are or were true; *when* or *whenever* can be used instead of *if*.

		Conditional (Present or Past Time)	Result (Present or Past Time)
		If I am sick,	*I drink a lot of tea.*
		If Maria needed to look up a word,	*she went to an online dictionary.*
Present	1.		
	2.		
Past	3.		
	4.		

3.15.8. With first conditionals, what verb forms/tenses are possible in the

if clause	result clause
_____	_____
_____	_____
_____	_____

3.15.9. Write three sentences with first conditionals. Remember that they are used for an action that is likely to happen. Vary the verb forms.

	Conditional (Future Time)	**Result (Future Time)**
	If it is cloudy,	*I won't go to the beach.*
1.		
2.		
3.		

3.15.10. With second conditionals, what verb forms/tenses are possible in the

if clause	result clause
_____	_____
_____	_____
_____	_____

3.15.11. Write three sentences with second conditionals. Remember that they are used for an action that is the speaker thinks is not very possible. Vary the verb forms.

	Conditional (Present or Future Time)	**Result (Present or Future Time)**
	If I had enough money,	*I would travel around the world.*
1.		
2.		
3.		

3.15.12. With third conditionals, what verb forms/tenses are possible in the

if clause	result clause
_____	_____
_____	_____
_____	_____

3.15.13. Write three sentences with third conditionals. Remember that they are used for an action that did not happen or the speaker wishes that did not happen.

	Conditional (Past Time)	**Result (Past Time)**
	If he had not been sick,	*he would not have missed the game.*
1.		
2.		
3.		

3.15.14. What is a mixed conditional?

_____

_____

3.15.15. Give three examples of sentences with mixed conditionals.

a. _____

_____

b. _____

_____

c. _____

_____

3.15.16. When is it possible to omit *if* in a conditional sentence? What happens when *if* is omitted?

_____

_____

3.15.17. Consider these two sentences. Why would ELLs have problems with them?

a. *He'd given up his job and moved to Colorado.*
b. *If he'd been more active, he wouldn't have gained so much weight.*

_____

_____

3.15.18. What does *wish* express? What is the grammar of *wish* and why is it difficult for ELLs?

_____

_____

_____

_____

3.15.19. Can you identify and explain these common ELL errors with this grammar point? Match the number of the type of error with its example.

Errors with Conditionals (*if* clauses) and *wish*

1. Don't use past tense to talk about past conditions.
2. Don't use present tense to talk about present time conditions.
3. When the verb **to be** is used in unreal conditions for actions in the present (or future), use **were** instead of **was** for all persons, singular and plural.
4. Remember that verbs in sentences with **wish** follow similar patterns to those for **if**. Wishing in the present time requires past tense, and wishing in the past time requires past perfect tense.

Student Errors

_____ a. *I would not trust that man if I was you.*

_____ b. *If she took the medicine last night that the doctor prescribed, she would have been able to go camping with us.*

_____ c. *I would join friends on their European trip if I have a valid passport.*

_____ d. *Matt wishes he has more time to study for tomorrow's test.*

_____ e. *Jorge and Anna would not move to the United States if the situation in their country was better at this time.*

_____ f. *If I have some free time, I would watch my favorite movies right now.*

_____ g. *I wish I knew that she was very sick. I would have visited her more often.*

_____ h. *Amy gets paid on the 1st of the month. Today is the 15th. If she can receive her paycheck today, she would buy a new suit she saw at the mall.*

_____ i. *I would buy another blue dress shirt if it was available.*

_____ j. *I would not have cooked dinner if I knew that you ordered pizza.*

_____ k. *If she spent her money reasonably last month, she would have had enough to pay rent.*

_____ l. *I wish Judy has a bigger car. I don't think her small car is safe.*

3.15.20. Find eight errors in conditionals *(if clauses)* and the use of *wish* in this student writing.

> *I am studying English in the U.S. right now, but I wish I was back*
>
> *home in Korea so that I could eat my mom's food every day. She makes the*
>
> *best bibimpab, stir fried vegetables with rice and beef. If I knew that I will*
>
> *miss her cooking so much, I would pay more attention when she was*
>
> *cooking. Food here is different. It is hard to find the right ingredients. I*
>
> *wish I have an Asian supermarket next to my house. If it was closer, I can*
>
> *go shopping there more often. I wish I have some Korean food right now.*

 ### Action Research Project to Inform Your Teaching

Examine a 500-word excerpt of a transcript of spoken English. Identify all of the conditional structures. How many of the structures have the main clause (i.e., the result clause with a form of *will* or *would*) but lack a directly stated *if* clause, such as *I would never have done that.*

PRACTICE FOR

4

Being on the Hot Seat:
Grammar Questions from ELLs

These 20 questions appear in Chapter 4 in the textbook *Keys to Teaching Grammar to English Language Learners*, followed by the answer. **Before you read any of Chapter 4 in the Handbook,** you should spend between five to ten minutes per question trying to sort out what you think the answer is before you actually check in the textbook.

Hot Seat Question 1. Which is correct: *a big house* or *a house big?* Why? (HB pp. 266–267)

_____

_____

_____

_____

_____

_____

Hot Seat Question 2. *Never has the weather been so cold!* I understand all the words in this sentence and the meaning, but the grammar looks strange to me. Why does the word *has* come before the subject *the weather*? Actually, this sentence looks more like a question than a statement: *Has the weather been so cold?* Why don't you say, *Never the weather has been so cold!* (HB pp. 267–268)

_____

_____

_____

_____

_____

_____

Hot Seat Question 3. When you add *–ing* or *–ed* to a word, how do you know how to spell the word? I mean, how do you know when to double the final consonant? Which is correct: *happening* or *happenning? opened* or *openned? prefered* or *preferred? begining* or *beginning?* (HB pp. 268–269)

_____

_____

_____

_____

_____

_____

Hot Seat Question 4. When do you use *used to?* I think it's for past tense, so what's the difference between simple past tense and *used to?* Does *I went to that school* mean the same as *I used to go to that school?* If they mean the same thing, is one form preferred? Is one slang? (HB pp. 269–270)

_____

_____

_____

_____

_____

_____

Hot Seat Question 5. *If I had a million dollars right now, I would buy a new house.* This sentence is talking about the present. That's what *right now* means. I don't understand how you can use *had* here because *had* is past tense, and this sentence is talking about the present. (HB pp. 270–271)

_____

_____

_____

_____

_____

Hot Seat Question 6. I saw a sentence with the word *had* two times in a row: *Before Lucas bought his classic 1973 Ford Mustang, he had had many other cars. However, not one of them was as nice as his Ford Mustang.* Is this really possible? What does *had had* mean? (HB pp. 271–272)

_____

_____

_____

_____

_____

Hot Seat Question 7. *I play usually tennis on Saturday morning with my doubles partner.* Is this sentence okay? Why or why not? My roommate is a native speaker, and she understands me when I say this, but my teacher says that this sentence is not right. (HB pp. 272–273)

_____

_____

_____

_____

_____

Hot Seat Question 8. I learned that I can't use *will* in an *if* clause, so I can't say, *If I will study harder, my grades will improve.* I'm supposed to use present tense and say, *If I study harder, my grades will improve.* The other day I heard a native speaker say, *If you will lend me $100, I will pay you back in a few days.* Is this sentence okay? Why or why not? (HB pp. 273–274)

_____

_____

_____

_____

_____

_____

Hot Seat Question 9. For the words *you are not*, I can say *you're not*, and I can also say *you aren't*. Is there any difference in these two? Are they both OK? (HB p. 274)

_____

_____

_____

_____

_____

_____

Hot Seat Question 10. *Did you ever work there?* When you ask a question about the past, why do you use the present form of a verb? (HB pp. 275–276)

_____

_____

_____

_____

_____

_____

Hot Seat Question 11. *I have lived here _____ two years.* Should I use *since* or *for* to fill in the blank? (HB p. 277)

_____

_____

_____

_____

_____

_____

Hot Seat Question 12. *Can you tell me where does Karen live?* My roommate told me that this sentence is wrong because I'm supposed to ask, *Can you tell me where Karen lives?* I thought that I needed to use *do/does/did* with questions. (HB pp. 277–278)

_____

_____

_____

_____

_____

_____

Hot Seat Question 13. I have a hard time with the word *other. Other* means "one more," so can I say, *I need other book now? Other* looks singular, but my teacher said you can use it with plural nouns like *other books.* What about *others?* I thought *others* is the plural form of *other. Others* looks plural, so why can't I say *others books* instead of *other books?* When do I use *other* and when do I use *others?* (HB pp. 278–279)

_____

_____

_____

_____

_____

_____

Hot Seat Question 14. *I feel good* or *I feel well.* Which one should I say when everyone asks me, *How are you doing?* (HB p. 279)

_____

_____

_____

_____

_____

_____

Hot Seat Question 15. Is *gonna* okay? If so, when can I use it? (HB pp. 280–281)

_____

_____

_____

_____

_____

_____

Hot Seat Question 16. Why do people ask me, *Have you ever eaten sushi?* with present perfect tense *(have eaten)* when they are asking about the past? Why do you use a tense named *present* to talk about the past? If you mean present time, then the person has to answer no about the sushi because I can see that he's not eating sushi now, and if he is eating sushi now, I think it would be stupid to ask someone if they are eating sushi. Do you see my point? (HB pp. 281–282)

_____

_____

_____

_____

_____

_____

Hot Seat Question 17. Which is correct: *boys'* or *boy's?* (HB pp. 282–283)

_____

_____

_____

_____

_____

_____

Hot Seat Question 18. How do I know when to add *–er* for comparison and when to use the word *more?* What's the secret trick? (HB pp. 283–284)

_____

_____

_____

_____

_____

_____

Hot Seat Question 19. What is the difference between *do* and *make?* Can I use one for the other? (HB pp. 284–285)

_____

_____

_____

_____

_____

Hot Seat Question 20. Which of these two sentences is correct? *I like very much tennis* or *I like tennis very much.* Is there any difference in meaning between these two sentences? (HB p. 286)

_____

_____

_____

_____

_____

_____

PRACTICE FOR

5

Specific Techniques for Teaching ELL Grammar

Exercise 5.1. Observing a Grammar Class (HB pp. 287–312)

One of the best ways to find out about different approaches to teaching grammar or any other aspect of ELL teaching is to observe a class. In some cases, you may observe a colleague, but sometimes it is preferable to observe teachers at a school with which you are not so familiar.

1. Choose a school, and ask permission to observe a class.

2. Attend the class.

3. Take notes during the class. A sample observation sheet is provided for you on pages 211–212, but you may use any recording device that you like. (Be sure to ask permission before recording any class.)

Here are some things that you could/should note as a good classroom observer:

a. What did the students do?

b. What did the teacher do?

c. How did the teacher begin the class?

d. How did the teacher end the class?

e. Did the teacher go over homework? If so, how?

f. Did the teacher check for student comprehension during the lesson? If so, how? Individually? As a group? Did the teacher say, "Did you understand?" or "Does anyone have any questions?" or did the teacher check comprehension by asking the students a question about the content?

g. Did the students work in pairs or groups? What did the teacher say in order to put the students in this arrangement?

h. How long did it take the students to rearrange themselves? In other words, was this a smooth transition or not? Why?

i. Did the students speak to each other in their L1? How frequently? Could you tell why they were doing this?

j. If the students spoke their native language, how did the teacher react to this? What do you think of student use of their L1 in class?

k. Did students use dictionaries during class? English-English or bilingual dictionaries? What did the teacher say/do about this?

4. Write one to two pages (double-spaced) reporting on your observation.

5. Send the teacher and/or director of the school a thank you note via email.

Class Observation

School: _____ Teacher: _____

Level/class: _____ Date:_____ Class time: _____

Textbook/workbook/pages covered: _____

Other materials (overhead, board):_____

Class size: _____ Student nationality/language: _____

Time	Type of Interaction T/S S/S T/C S	Book Page	Language Point	Observation	Reaction/ comment

Time	Type of Interaction T/S S/S T/C S	Book Page	Grammar Point	Observation	Reaction/ comment

Exercise 5.2. Implementing a New Technique in Your Class (HB pp. 287–312)

The ultimate test of how a technique works is for you to try it out in your own class. In this case, you should keep a journal of what you planned to happen, what happened, and how the class went. It is important to have a record of what you thought would happen so that you can accurately compare this with what actually happened.

1. Which of the techniques in Chapter 5 (or from elsewhere) are you going to implement?

   _____

   _____

   _____

2. Why did you choose this technique?

   _____

   _____

   _____

   _____

3. What is your plan? Which lesson (grammar point) will you implement this technique with?

   _____

   _____

4. Have you ever done anything similar to this in your teaching?

   _____

   _____

   _____

5. How do you think your students will react to this technique?

   _____

   _____

   _____

After the Lesson:

6. What actually happened during the class?

_____

_____

_____

_____

_____

_____

_____

_____

7. Reflect on the class. What is your reaction?

_____

_____

_____

_____

_____

_____

8. In hindsight, what could you or should you have changed, if anything?

_____

_____

_____

_____

_____

_____

Answers for Exercises

Chapter 1 (pages 1–16)

Exercise 1.01 (page 1)

1. ELL; Global warming <u>could to harm</u> (could harm) our planet forever. We <u>must to act</u> (must act) now.
2. NS; If you <u>would have</u> (had) considered more information, perhaps you would be working in a very different place today.
3. ELL; The meeting began promptly <u>in</u> (at) noon.
4. ELL; Most historians agree that George Washington <u>was great</u> (was a great) president.
5. NS; Let's take <u>them</u> (those) boxes to the car now before it rains.
6. NS; I don't think our decision will <u>effect</u> (affect) anyone really.
7. ELL; When did you get married <u>with</u> (to) him?
8. ELL; The most important thing in <u>the life</u> (life) <u>is the friendship</u> (is friendship).
9. NS; The program that my company uses today to prevent consumer fraud was invented by Jonathan Spears and <u>myself</u> (me) in 2004.
10. ELL; Turkey is the place that I would like to <u>visit it in</u> (visit in) the near future.
11. ELL; The police are not sure about when the <u>accident was happened</u> (accident happened).
12. NS; If you're not feeling well, then you should <u>lay</u> (lie) down for a little while.
13. NS; He was completely surprised. You should have <u>saw</u> (seen) his face.
14. NS; There are <u>kitten's</u> (kittens) for sale at that house.

Exercise 1.02 (page 2)

1. NS; I wish I had <u>went</u> (gone) to your party. I hear it was a huge success.
2. ELL; When I was <u>shave</u> (shaving) today, I cut myself just above my upper lip.
3. NS; The best decorated house belongs to the <u>Smiths'</u> (Smiths) without any doubt.
4. ELL; The teacher decided to put off <u>to give</u> (giving) us the exam until next week.
5. NS; Columbus couldn't sail on <u>no</u> (any) more trips because he didn't have money.
6. NS; The prize will go to <u>whomever</u> (whoever) has the most points at the end of 20 minutes of play.
7. ELL; Luke won the prize. In every competition, he <u>always has</u> (is always) lucky.
8. NS; Between you and <u>I</u> (me), there is no reason to rush to finish this project now.
9. ELL; My car is not <u>run</u> (running) well today. I'm not sure what is wrong.
10. NS; We should <u>of</u> (have) watched the weather report last night to find out the chance of rain for today.
11. NS; Could you tell me where Jacob <u>lives at</u> (lives)?
12. ELL; Swallowtail butterflies can be recognized by their unique <u>colorment</u> (color OR coloring).
13. ELL; To complete this task successfully, each of you will need more equipments (equipment) and supplies.
14. ELL; If you have any extra scraps of material, do not <u>throw away them</u> (throw them away). Give them to us so they can be recycled.

Exercise 1.03 Answering ELL Grammar Questions (page 3)
Working individually and then with a partner, answer these questions asked by ELLs.
1. See pages 278–279 in the Handbook.
2. Yes, you can say *had had*. See pages 271–272 in the Handbook.
3. See pages 282–283 in the Handbook.

Exercise 1.04 (page 4)
Answers will vary.

Exercise 1.05 (page 4)
Dear Teacher,

Tomorrow <u>start English classes</u> (English classes start), and I am really excited <u>for</u> (about) that. I have a <u>questions</u> (question) for you. My son <u>has</u> (is) 15 years old, and he is <u>in</u> (on) vacation from school now. He has to return to Brazil in February, and I would like to invite him to our class just for a <u>little</u> (few) days. He <u>speak</u> (speaks) English, but he needs (to) practice more. I really believe that this <u>classes</u> (class) is just what he needs.

Is (it) possible for him to attend this class?

Explanations:
Subjects (*classes*) precede verbs (*start*).
We say *excited about*. This is an adjective + preposition combination.
Questions should be singular to go with *a*.
We say *on* vacation, not *in*. Preposition usage is difficult.
We use *a few* with count nouns like *days*.
We say *speaks* for subject-verb agreement.
We usually need *to* between two verbs such as *need* and *practice*.
We are talking about one class, so we say *class*, not *classes*. Also, *this* is singular and requires *class*.
We need a subject (*it*) for the verb *is: Is it possible . . . ?*

Exercise 1.06 (page 5)

(<u>The</u>) Dominican Republic and Haiti

(<u>The</u>) Dominican Republic is a country located <u>at</u> (in) the Caribbean. This nation <u>share</u> (shares) one island with Haiti. <u>both</u> (Both) are <u>nations</u> <u>poors</u> (poor nations), but (the) Dominican Republic <u>have</u> (has) <u>two third</u> (two-thirds) of the island, and its natural resources are more <u>accessibles</u> (accessible) than <u>the Haiti</u> (Haiti's) natural resources. The economy in Haiti is not so good, so this <u>make</u> (makes) the <u>haitian</u> (Haitian) population <u>to move</u> (move) to (the) Dominican Republic in order to get prosperity. This economic situation <u>force</u> (forces) them to cross the frontier and stay <u>iligaly</u> (illegally) in (the) Dominican Republic, generating a problem similar to the <u>actual</u> (current) <u>ilegal</u> (illegal) <u>inmigration</u> (immigration) we have in the <u>Unite State</u> (United States) of America.

Explanations:
Some country names need *the*: the Dominican Republic.
We say *in* the Caribbean because it refers to an area.
We say *shares* for subject-verb agreement.
Both needs a capital letter because it is the first word of a sentence.
We say *poor nations* because adjectives go before nouns and do not have plural forms.
We say *has* for subject-verb agreement.
Two-thirds is the correct way to express this fraction.
We say *accessible* because adjectives do not have plural forms.
We say *Haiti's* because we need a possessive form here.
We say *makes* for subject-verb agreement.
Haitian needs a capital letter because it is a proper noun.

We say *move* because verbs after *let, make,* and *have* are in the simple (base) form.
We say *forces* for subject-verb agreement.
Illegally is a spelling error.
We say *current*, not *actual*. (This is a false cognate from Spanish.)
Illegal and *immigration* are spelling errors.

The student wrote *Unite State* without /s/ because in his dialect of Spanish, a post-syllabic /s/ is not aspirated. (This applies to Spanish spoken in most of Central America, all of the Caribbean including coastal areas of Colombia and Venezuela, and certain other areas of South America but mostly in coastal areas.)

Exercise 1.07 (page 6)
Answers will vary.

Exercise 1.08 (page 7)
Answers will vary.

Exercise 1.09 (page 7)
Answers will vary.

Exercise 1.10 (page 8)
Old MacDonald had (E) a farm (C), (B)
E-I-E-I-O
And on his (A) farm (C) (D) he (A) had (E) a cow (C), (B)
E-I-E-I-O
With a "moo-moo" (C) here
and a "moo-moo" (C) there
Here a "moo" (C)
there a "moo" (C)
Everywhere a "moo-moo" (C)
Old MacDonald had (E) a farm (C), (B)
E-I-E-I-O

Exercise 1.11 (page 9)
A student (C) wants (A) to find out the kind (C) of soil that can hold (B) the most <u>water</u> (N). She buys (A) four identical pots with small holes in the bottom (C) of each. She then fills (A) each pot (C) with a different kind (C) of soil and <u>waters</u> (A) (V) the pots with the exact same amount (C) of <u>water</u> (N). How can she determine (B) the amount (C) of <u>water</u> (N) that stays (A) in the soil in each pot (C)?

A. By putting (E) cotton in each pot (C) to see how much <u>water</u> (N) it absorbs (A).
B. By carefully examining (E) the growth of flowers in each of the pots.
C. By covering (E) only three of the pots with a plastic bag (C).
D. By measuring (E) how much <u>water</u> (N) drains (A) from each pot (C).
Answers to F: *soil, water, cotton, growth*

Exercise 1.12 (page 10)
Answers will vary.

Exercise 1.13 (page 11)
1. B; verb tenses; modals
2. D; verb tenses; active vs. passive voice
3. B; possessive adjectives
4. D; verb tenses; verb forms
5. B; articles

Exercise 1.14 (page 12)

1a. C 1b. mainly *on*
2a. C 2b. *quietly*
3a. B 3b. *Listening*
4. 1a and 1b: B; 2a and 2b: A; 3a and 3b: C
5. Answers will vary. Suggested: In some ways, the error identification questions allow the tester to examine more grammar material with the same number of questions. In this case, a multiple choice question can cover one grammar point, but the corresponding error identification question can cover four grammar points.
6. Answers will vary. In general, ELLs find the error identification more difficult because there are four questions, not just one. In addition, these errors are probably errors that students actually make, but in some cases, all four answer options in a multiple choice question may not include three errors that ELLs actually make. In other words, sometimes the test writer feels compelled to have four options, so the distractor options may vary in how accurately they reflect *real* ELL errors.

Exercise 1.15 (page 13)

Answers will vary.

Exercise 1.16 (page 14)

Answers will vary.

Exercise 1.17 (page 15–16)

My Friend

The most (funnies) (consonant cluster of /–st/ not heard in speech) thing that Ryan has done is when he was wakebording and one guy that was wakebording to (fall out) (fell off: prepositions are often very hard to catch exactly in normal speech) of his wakeboard and Ryan was coming (bihind) (spelling the way it sounds) him꜀ and Ryan jumped over his head꜀ and the guy got scared and screamed "(wach) (spelling the way it sounds) out꜀" and Ryan just (laugh) (not hearing the /t/). (Note that the tone of this paragraph is more like a conversation instead of a more traditional written paragraph. In fact, note the lack of punctuation. The student is writing what he has heard from his friends. The teaching point is that CALP and BICS have very different language features and structures. They are not just formal and informal versions of English.)

The (things) (*things* is a conversation word and is not commonly found in good writing) that Ryan likes is to wakeboard and (R)ide (Q)uads.

Ryan was named after (a) (a/an not heard clearly in rapid spoken English) Irish (dancer, Ryan) (fused sentence represents spoken language) was born in Woodland. He is 14 years old.

Ryan has moved a (lot he) (run-on sentence represents spoken language) lived in Chico, Waveland, Summerville, Ocala, Woodland and (Richland, Ryan) (fused sentence represents spoken language) is living in Waveland right know.

Ryan likes to (wakeboard hes) (run-on sentence represents spoken language) (ben) (*hes ben* is just as it sounds) wakebording since he was 12 years old. Ryan also likes to ride quads and he (rases) (just as it sounds) all over the place and (hes) (just as it sounds) been riding quads since he was 5 years old and he rides a Honda 450 and hes (just as it sounds) won a lot of (*a lot of* is common in spoken language, but textbooks would use *many*, *numerous*, or *several*—not *a lot of*) 1st place (trophis) (how it sounds). (This last compilation of 39 words should be several sentences, not one. This huge run-on sentence represents good spoken language but is not good written language.)

Ryan wants to go to UMC college (thas) (how it sounds) located in Chico. Ryan wants to be a criminal (justce) (just as it sounds) police.

Ryan wants to work (like) (overuse of like instead of *as*; *as* is hard to pick up in rapid conversation but *like* stands out) a coast guard when he (grows) (grow up: prepositions are often very hard to catch exactly in normal speech).

The other thing that Ryan wants to be is a pro racer for quads or dirtbikes, the (most worst thing) (sounds very conversational: *the most worst* is double superlative and *thing* is not good academic writing, but it is what this ELL constantly hears) that had (happen) (difficult to hear the /d/) to him is that he broke his (helment) (spelling error) in half in (a) (*a/an* is delivered so quickly that it is hard to catch the correct usage) accident he had when he was racing he only had a few (brewses) (as it sounds) and (thats) (as it sounds) it but he still races (until) (to: prepositions are often very hard to catch exactly in normal speech) this day. (This huge sentence is one paragraph. This run-on sentence represents good spoken language but is not good written language.)

Ryan's favorite people (is) (subject-verb agreement) Eric (Murphay) (spelling error) and James (Stuward) (final consonant /d/ or /t/ is very difficult to catch exactly in normal speech). Eric Murphay is a (profecional) (spelling error) wake border and James (stuwars) (final consonant /d/ or /t/ is very difficult to catch exactly in normal speech) is a (profecional) (spelling error) dirtbiker.

Chapter 2 (pages 17–93)

Exercise 2.01 (page 17)
Boxes checked yes: 1,2,5,6,7,8,10
Boxes checked no: 3,4,9

Exercise 2.02 (page 18)
1. between you and *me*
2. James, Laura, and *I*
3. Correct
4. Tim, Rodrigo, and *me*
5. my husband and *me*
6. Correct
7. my brother and *me*
8. my sister and *I*
9. Correct
10. people like Ed and *me*

Exercise 2.03 (page 19)
1. so John and *I*
2. Correct
3. As for *me*
4. for Kelly and *me*
5. both Ian and *I*
6. Correct
7. to make *me* feel
8. for *me*
9. spend hours with *me*
10. Correct

Exercise 2.04 (page 20)
1. could have *taken*
2. should have *done*
3. could have *drunk*
4. Correct
5. would have *gone*
6. Correct
7. she *saw*
8. is *broken*
9. Correct
10. had he *known*

Exercise 2.05 (page 21)
1. laid
2. lie
3. lying
4. lay
5. laying
6. lying
7. lain
8. lying
9. laid
10. lain

Exercise 2.06 (page 22)
1. *whoever* told you
2. *who* knows
3. Correct
4. *whom* my husband and I
5. Correct
6. *whom* they should
7. persons *who* are responsible
8. *whoever* wants to have them
9. one person *whom*
10. Correct

Exercise 2.07 (page 23)
1. doesn't
2. doesn't
3. doesn't
4. Correct
5. doesn't
6. Correct
7. doesn't
8. Correct
9. doesn't
10. doesn't

Exercise 2.08 (page 24)
1. Joe *had* not just spent
2. if I *had* known
3. if I *had* accepted it
4. Correct

5. if they *had* not attended
6. Correct
7. if the committee members *had* not known
8. if Andres *had* not brought
9. Correct
10. if my husband *had* had

Exercise 2.09 (page 25)
1. Correct
2. I don't have *a/any* problem
3. does not have *any* food
4. I can't seem to find *any* of them
5. no one has *ever*
6. Correct
7. Correct
8. had *any* time
9. with *anything* anyone else says
10. or email me *any* more

Exercise 2.10 (page 26)
1. badly
2. Correct
3. Correct
4. badly
5. bad
6. badly
7. Correct
8. bad
9. bad
10. badly

Exercise 2.11 (page 27)
1. Correct
2. *those* words
3. *those* clouds
4. *those* families
5. Correct
6. *those* bulbs
7. *those* other shoes
8. *those* biscuits
9. *those* results
10. Correct

Exercise 2.12 (page 28)
1. should *have* stayed
2. Correct
3. might *have* done
4. would *have* called
5. must *have* attacked
6. might *have* done
7. must *have* been devastated
8. Correct
9. Correct
10. should *have* fired

Exercise 2.13 (page 29)
1. It's
2. Its
3. it's
4. its
5. its
6. it's
7. Its
8. It's
9. its
10. It's

Exercise 2.14 (page 29)

Have you ever been to Venice? I think that <u>your</u> spirits will be lifted by visiting Venice. Most tourists arrive in Venice by train. As you step out of the railway station, right away <u>you're</u> facing the Canal Grande, its main water artery. After wandering the small *campi* (parts) of Venice, crossing bridge after bridge, you will soon find yourself at another magnificent spectacle, Saint Mark's Square, where <u>you're</u> made aware of how small and insignificant <u>you're</u> feeling at this moment in comparison to the ageless beauty of the square and its central masterpiece, Saint Mark's Cathedral.

Your impression of Venice changes after dark. With waves of tourists gone, piazzas are breathing again, gondolas slowly moving on the water, and on Saint Mark's Square, the bands start their nightly competition for <u>your</u> attention, playing music from all over the world.

Don't try to see Venice in one day. Allow it to reveal itself. You'll be surprised and rewarded with side trips to the islands of Murano and Burano, which are world famous for their glass-blowing factories and lace, respectively. When it comes to a visit to Venice, your age does not matter because there is something here for people of all ages. It does not matter how many times you have visited *la serenissima repubblica di Venezia* (the Most Serene Republic of Venice, as it was once called). It always seems to call you back, and soon <u>you're</u> waiting for that next trip as if it were <u>your</u> first. You're certainly in for a real treat in this great city.

Exercise 2.15 (page 30)

One day a driver was taking a truckload of <u>penguins</u> from the airport to the zoo. The penguins had just arrived in the city from the North Pole. On the way to the zoo, the truck's radiator overheated, and the driver was trying to figure out how to get the penguins to their destination as quickly as possible. The truck <u>driver's</u> requests for a repair truck were getting no reply, so he was in a bit of a panic.

He flagged down a van that was passing by. The truck driver pleaded with the van driver for help. "Here's $100 to take these penguins to the zoo. Can you do this?"

The van driver's response was an immediate "Yes, certainly." Through the <u>drivers'</u> amazing teamwork, they transferred the penguins to the van in a matter of minutes, and then the van driver started driving toward the zoo.

A repair truck finally showed up and took care of the truck's mechanical problem. After his truck was fixed, the truck driver drove as fast as he could to the zoo to make sure the penguins were all right. As he got near the zoo, he was shocked to see the van full of penguins driving away from the zoo. The truck driver turned around his truck and drove as fast as he could to catch up with the van. He flashed his lights and honked his horn to get the van driver to pull over to the side of the road.

The truck driver got out of his truck and walked over to the van. "What are you doing? I gave you $100 to take the penguins to the zoo!" The van <u>driver's</u> calm response explained it all: "I did take them to the zoo, but we had about $35 left over, so I thought I'd take them to the park now."

Exercise 2.16 (page 31)
1. who's
2. whose
3. Correct
4. Correct
5. who's
6. whose
7. who's
8. who's
9. who's
10. Correct

Exercise 2.17 (page 32)
1. to
2. to
3. to
4. to
5. too
6. to
7. to
8. two
9. to
10. too
11. to
12. to
13. to
14. too
15. two
16. to

Exercise 2.18 (page 33)
1. affected
2. effects
3. Correct
4. effect
5. Correct
6. affected
7. Correct
8. effect
9. effects
10. affected

Exercise 2.19 (page 34)
1. lose
2. Correct
3. lose
4. loose
5. Correct
6. loose
7. lose
8. loose
9. Correct
10. lose

Exercise 2.20 (page 35)

   Arguably, college years are the best in anyone's life. In some countries, students live care-free lives, partying as much as they can, and all <u>they're</u> expected to do is attend classes and do well. There are countries in the world where students do not have part-time jobs or rent to pay. They live with <u>their</u> parents until they graduate or even until they get married. <u>Their</u> parents pay for <u>their</u> education even if the family is not very well off. In the United States, things are a bit different. Sometimes students not only go to school full-time but also manage to juggle a couple of part-time jobs. It is obvious that the quality of their college work might suffer from such tight schedules, but <u>they're</u> paying rent and other bills and are therefore forced to priori-tize. Wouldn't it be great if students getting a college education did not need to worry about <u>their</u> bills, loans, and other financial responsibilities? So many young minds and hours would be freed and could be used to benefit the world. This may be a bit idealistic, but <u>there</u> is always hope.

Exercise 2.21 (page 36)
1. had known; money problems
2. Andrea and I; never laid
3. he doesn't; feel bad
4. It's; two small
5. drunk; taste bad
6. doesn't; who's hungry
7. smoke affects; they're
8. lose; should have been
9. Where are we meeting?; any of the packages
10. I should have driven; It's

Exercise 2.22 (page 37)

Let's review. By now, you should <u>have</u> been made aware of 20 native speaker grammar mistakes. Some of these errors are more common and unfortunately occur <u>too</u> often in writing and speaking. As a teacher, <u>you're</u> a prime example for your ELLs, so your use of correct grammar should extend far beyond this book. Imagine if you had a teacher <u>who</u> made grammar mistakes. Would you <u>lose</u> respect for that instructor? Wouldn't you feel <u>bad</u>? <u>It's</u> hard to imagine such a thing until you put yourself in your <u>students'</u> shoes. As a teacher, you are a person <u>who's</u> responsible for the accuracy of the information <u>they're</u> getting. That you are not very sure about the rules yet <u>doesn't</u> matter. Practice and experience will help. <u>Teachers</u> have a profound <u>effect</u> on each <u>student's</u> learning. <u>It's</u> up to you to do the best job possible to help <u>those</u> learners. If not you, then <u>who</u>?

Exercise 2.23 (page 38)

Riddle 1. cats, box, cat, kittens, copycats.
Riddle 2. dog, circles, watchdog, winding.
Riddle 3. cat, computer, mouse, marks.
Riddle 4. dog, flea market.

Exercise 2.24 (page 38)

 1. PL
 2. V
 3. PL
 4. PL
 5. PL
 6. PL
 7. PL
 8. PL
 9. V
10. PL
11. POSS
12. V
13. PL
14. V
15. PL
16. V
17. PL
18. V
19. PL
20. V
21. POSS
22. V
23. POSS
24. PL
25. V
26. PL
27. PL
28. PL
29. V
30. POSS

Exercise 2.25 (page 39)

 1. 3: illnesses
 2. 7: Maple Street
 3. 5: a loaf
 4. 1: problems
 5. 2: country
 6. 4: homework
 7. 6: believe life
 8. 5: a movie (or 1: movies)
 9. 1: earthquakes
10. 4: furniture
11. 7: September
12. 6: have real talent
13. 5: a fax
14. 1: months
15. 2: student

Exercise 2.26 (page 40)

These stunning bird's eye <u>views</u> offer rare and beautiful <u>glimpses</u> of West Michigan's <u>rivers</u>, <u>lakes</u>, and <u>shoreline</u> from the lofty <u>perch</u> of the camera <u>lens</u> of <u>Marge Beaver</u>. Her breathtaking four-season <u>photographs</u> transform our <u>view</u> of <u>Michigan</u> into a magical <u>land</u>. From the working <u>harbors</u> and <u>lights</u> along <u>Lake Michigan</u>, to the playful inland <u>lakes</u>, to the fruit-covered <u>orchards</u>, spectacular <u>flowers</u>, and fun-filled <u>festivals</u>, these are <u>images</u> of <u>Michigan</u> as you've never seen her before. All of these, plus arresting <u>photographs</u> of winding <u>highways</u>, snake-like <u>rivers</u>, and city <u>harbors</u> make this <u>book</u> a collector's <u>item</u> for anyone who loves this beautiful <u>state</u>.

Exercise 2.27 (page 40)
1. trial—CONC, Justice—ABST, betrayal—ABST, deceit—ABST, taxpayers—CONC, million—CONC
2. James—CONC, attention—ABST, details—CONC, dedication—ABST, respect—ABST, colleagues—CONC
3. Patience—ABST, virtue—ABST
4. Maria—CONC, way—CONC, relaxation—ABST, stress—ABST, office—CONC, yoga—CONC, week—CONC
5. joke—CONC, people—CONC
6. child—CONC, curiosity—ABST, trouble—ABST, places—CONC, house—CONC
7. way—CONC, peace—ABST, honesty—ABST
8. talent—ABST, work—ABST, luck—ABST
9. Helena—CONC, husband—CONC, success—ABST, album—CONC, piano—CONC
10. pride—ABST, friendship—ABST

Exercise 2.28 (page 41)
1. cloud—C, lining—C
2. charity—NC, home—C
3. smoke—NC, fire—NC
4. money—NC
5. dogs—C
6. gold—NC
7. eggs—C, basket—C
8. Silence—NC

Exercise 2.29 (page 41)

In this intriguing article, Christinson <u>talks</u> about brain-research application for ESL classroom. She <u>emphasizes</u> the importance of the limbic system and students' emotional self-regulation for teaching. She <u>describes</u> four pathways of recalling information: procedural, episodic, semantic, and sensory. She <u>explains</u> that episodic memory <u>provides</u> important clues concerning the retention of information as people usually <u>remember</u> emotionally hooked events, which <u>can be</u> successfully used in teaching. Semantic memory <u>is</u> of no less importance because it <u>is used</u> for remembering concepts and general knowledge, which <u>does</u> not <u>depend</u> on the context. Then she <u>addresses</u> factors which <u>affect</u> attention such as novelty, need, emotion, and meaning. The author <u>notes</u> that emotion <u>is</u> a key factor in both attention and learning. The brain <u>is</u> a pattern-seeking device, and each student's brain <u>constructs</u> a unique meaning.

Exercise 2.30 (page 42)
1. 7: enjoyed
2. 4: Whom did you
3. 1: I am twenty
4. 8: bought it
5. 2: makes
6. 9: they might want
7. 5: are looking
8. 3: don't like
9. 5: are you doing
10. 9: could take
11. 1: are
12. 3: does not come
13. 6: has taken
14. 6: have visited
15. 6: have lived

Exercise 2.31 (page 43)
Answers will vary.

Exercise 2.32 (page 44)
1. is, remains
2. sounds
3. turned
4. looked
5. seemed
6. smells, tastes
7. became, was
8. None

Exercise 2.33 (page 45)
1. has (AUX) been (V), have (AUX) done (V)
2. am (AUX), has (V), am (V), do (V), is (V), have (AUX)
3. are (AUX), have (V)
4. has (V), is (V), does (AUX), do (V)
5. is (AUX)
6. is (V), 've (AUX), been (AUX), do (V)
7. does (AUX), is (V), has (V)
8. were (AUX), live (V), have (AUX), had (V)
9. did (V), did (AUX), do (V), did (V)
10. is (V), has (V)

Exercise 2.34 (page 46)

There <u>was</u> (V) a huge psychiatrists' convention in town for the week. One afternoon, after they <u>had</u> (AUX) attended numerous sessions, three psychiatrists <u>had</u> (AUX) <u>had</u> (V) enough of the conference and decided to go out for a walk.

The first one said, "You know, people <u>are</u> (AUX) always coming to us with all of their problems, but I never <u>have</u> (V) a chance to tell anyone about my issues."

The other two concurred, and one of them said, "Hey, why don't we each tell what <u>is</u> (AUX) bothering us? We<u>'re</u> (V) all professionals, so we <u>have</u> (V) the skills to help each other, right?" They all agreed that this <u>was</u> (V) a great idea.

The first psychiatrist confessed, "I <u>have</u> (AUX) <u>been</u> (AUX) hiding something for most of my adult life. I <u>am</u> (V) a compulsive shopper. I <u>am</u> (AUX) always shopping for things in stores and online. I <u>am</u> (V) completely in debt, and I <u>am</u> (AUX) forced to charge my patients exorbitant fees so I can make ends meet."

The second psychiatrist began, "I <u>have</u> (AUX) <u>had</u> (V) a drug problem for years. In fact, it<u>'s</u> (V) completely out of control, and it<u>'s</u> (AUX) ruining my life. I don't know how much longer I can bear to keep this secret."

The third said, "I know that it<u>'s</u> (V) wrong, but no matter how hard I try, I just cannot keep a secret."

Exercise 2.35 (page 47)

When you are thinking about purchasing a car, a few things <u>should</u> be considered. First of all, you need to know how far you <u>would</u> drive the car and how big it <u>ought</u> to be. If you are a family of four or more, a mini-van <u>might</u> be an option, but having that kind of a vehicle <u>will</u> not leave much money in your wallet with current gas prices. Some people <u>might</u> favor foreign cars and consider some Japanese models to be among the most reliable, economical, and long lasting ones. You <u>may</u> want to visit a few dealerships before you make a final decision. In addition, smart shoppers <u>should</u> do research online these days and walk into the dealership with a clear picture of what is needed in order to save time and money. Buying a car <u>could</u> take up a few hours of your time, so you <u>must</u> not buy a car when you are tired. It is a considerable investment and <u>can</u> turn into a nightmare if you end up with something you do not really like. However, there is no greater feeling than driving your new car home knowing that you did all you <u>could</u> to find the best deal in town.

Exercise 2.36 (page 48)

1. 7
2. 1
3. 6
4. 2
5. 5
6. 3
7. 1
8. 4
9. 2
10. 5
11. 3
12. 6
13. 4
14. 7
15. 4
16. 3
17. 5
18. 2
19. 6
20. 1

7. 4
8. 1
9. 3
10. 5
11. 1
12. 2
13. 4
14. 2
15. 3
16. 5
17. 4
18. 2
19. 3
20. 1

Exercise 2.37 (page 49)

1. she (1), it (2), she (1), it (2)
2. me (2), I (1), myself (5), they (1), me (2)
3. he (1), his (7), he (1)
4. Nothing (4), me (2), this (6)
5. you (1), something (4), it (1), what (3), it (2)

Exercise 2.38 (page 49)

1. 3
2. 4
3. 5
4. 1
5. 5
6. 2

Exercise 2.39 (page 50)

1. an old blue plastic dollhouse
2. six tiny multi-colored Japanese paper frogs
3. a small antique wooden table
4. a shiny 19th-century silver Russian pendant
5. a new round rubber ball

Exercise 2.40 (page 50)

1. 4; snowy
2. 4; historical
3. 1; good things
4. 2; beautiful
5. 3; bigger
6. 1; dangerous situation
7. 4; interesting
8. 1; the most exciting park
9. 3; better
10. 2; nice
11. 4; married
12. 2; great

Exercise 2.41 (page 51)

After years of delivering pizzas, selling shoes, and waiting tables, a (ART) young (DESC) businessman had saved enough (DESC) money to start his (POSS) own (DESC) business. He rented a (ART) beautiful (DESC) office and got the (ART) best (DESC) decorations that he could for his (POSS) new (DESC) place. Sitting there, he saw a (ART) man come into the (ART) outer (DESC) office. The (ART) businessman wanted to look busy (DESC), as if his (POSS) office were really doing well, so he picked up the (ART) phone and started to pretend that he was working on a (ART) big (DESC) international (DESC) deal. He was shouting incredibly huge (DESC) figures and making giant (DESC) proposals to buy and trade stocks. The (ART) second (DESC) guy just stood there. He couldn't help overhearing everything.

Finally, the (ART) businessman hung up and asked the (ART) silent (DESC) visitor, "Can I help you?" The (ART) rather timid (DESC) visitor said, "Sure. I'm here to install your (POSS) new (DESC) phone."

Exercise 2.42 (page 51)
1. ADV
2. ADJ
3. V
4. V
5. ADJ
6. ADV
7. ADV
8. V
9. V
10. ADJ

Exercise 2.43 (page 52)
1. never; how often
2. here; where
3. quickly; how
4. tomorrow; when
5. equally; how much
6. so; how much
7. quite; how much
8. very; how much

Exercise 2.44 (page 52)
1. 1
2. 2
3. 1
4. 3
5. 2
6. 1
7. 3
8. 2
9. 1
10. 3
11. 2
12. 2
13. 3
14. 1
15. 1
16. 3
17. 2
18. 2
19. 3
20. 1

Exercise 2.45 (page 53)
1. 1; cleverly
2. 2; quickly asked
3. 2; never forget him
4. 4; provide a lot of assistance
5. 3; to the question with difficulty
6. 5; TV a lot
7. 5; a great deal
8. 2; have already
9. 5; badly

10. 1; rarely
11. 2; is always willing
12. 1; extremely
13. 5; really like it OR like it a lot
14. 2; utterly uninhabitable
15. 3; carefully

Exercise 2.46 (page 54)
1. P
2. P
3. C
4. C
5. P
6. C
7. C
8. P
9. C
10. C
11. C
12. C

Exercise 2.47 (page 55)
1. 1
2. 3
3. 1
4. 2
5. 2
6. 1
7. 3
8. 3
9. 2
10. 2
11. 1
12. 2
13. 3
14. 2
15. 3
16. 1
17. 2
18. 3
19. 1
20. 1

Exercise 2.48 (page 56)
1. 1; Grand Canyon, so this
2. 4; answers will vary
3. 2; father, but he continues
4. 3; brave, you
5. 3; shopping, but OR shopping; however, her
6. 2; tomorrow, I will
7. 4; answers will vary
8. 2; raining, we
9. 2; stubborn, I continued
10. 3; so tall, it was

11. 4; answers will vary
12. 4; airport because
13. 3; test, she failed
14. 2; dirty, so his mother
15. 1; Because she was late (OR: late, so we)

Exercise 2.49 (page 57)

<u>Although</u> [2] <u>both</u> ESL <u>and</u> [3] EFL students are learning English, those who teach English to non-native speakers know that methods used in ESL classrooms are not always suitable for EFL ones. In her article, Mary Black explained how ESL methodology is adapted to EFL environment at the Institute of North American Studies (INAS) in Barcelona, Spain, where strong emphasis is made on sharing information orally <u>and</u> [1] less on written communication. At INAS, classes are focused on listening <u>and</u> [1] speaking <u>because</u> [2] students can do reading <u>and</u> [1] writing in the form of <u>either</u> journals <u>or</u> [3] movie reports for homework. EFL students are not exposed to correct English as much as ESL learners are, <u>so</u> [1] it is imperative that they learn correct grammar. Teachers provide explicit grammar instruction, check comprehension, <u>and</u> [1] reinforce structure acquisition with clear board work. Students <u>not only</u> have written output <u>but also</u> [3] practice speaking. Finally, Black pointed out the importance of communication <u>and</u> [1] grammar combination. Grammar activities should be <u>both</u> communicative <u>and</u> [3] focused on structure learning as well.

Exercise 2.50 (page 57)

1. at – L, at – T, on – T
2. at – T, After –T, at – L, From – M, to – M
3. to – M, by –T, for – T
4. After – T, to – M, for – T
5. on – T, from – M, to – M

Exercise 2.51 (page 58)

1. 4, including
2. 1, in August
3. 3, listen to music
4. 2, in her car
5. 5, impression on everyone
6. 2, lived in Caracas
7. 3, regardless of the circumstances
8. 5, dependent on my parents
9. 5, hearts in(to) their songs
10. 1, school in 2005
11. 2, daughter at Little Book Academy
12. 4, a dozen reasons (OR: dozens of reasons
13. 1, on Mondays
14. 5, believe in ghosts
15. 3, thank you for all your help

Exercise 2.52 (page 59)

Correction is an issue (of concern) (for ESL and EFL teachers). Considerable research has been done (in the past decades) (on the subject). Some researchers believe that learners should be free to produce typical overgeneralization errors (for L2 structures). Others state that the lack (of correction) might imply (to the learner) that an incorrect production is correct. They believe correction is necessary (at some point) (in a learner's L2 development). Many researchers agree that if students recognize that they are making errors, it should help them realize that they need to continue their learning. There is no doubt that to benefit (from correction) learners need to know that they are being corrected. Immediate correction allows students to notice the difference (between their version (of the L2) and correct production).

Exercise 2.53 (page 59)
1a. V; 1b. N; 1c. Adj; 2a. V; 2b. Adj; 2c. N;
3a. Adj; 3b. V; 3c. N; 4a. N; 4b. Adj; 4c. V;
5a. Adj; 5b. N; 5c. V

Exercise 2.54 (page 60)
Answers will vary.

Exercise 2.55 (page 61)
1. Adj
2. Adj
3. Adv
4. Adj
5. N
6. N
7. N
8. N
9. Adv
10. N
11. Prep
12. Adj
13. Adj
14. Conj
15. Adv
16. Conj
17. Adj
18. N
19. N
21. Pro

Exercise 2.56 (page 62)
1. N
2. Adj

3. V
4. Conj
5. V
6. Adv
7. Prep
8. Adj
9. Conj
10. Adj
11. Adv
12. V
13. N
14. Prep
15. Adj
16. Prep
17. N
18. V
19. N
20. Adv

Exercise 2.57 (page 62)
Answers will vary.

Exercise 2.58 (page 63)
1. /is
2. /describes
3. /are
4. /vividly
5. /also
6. /illustrates
7. /describes
8. /is built

Exercise 2.59 (page 64)

Each <u>chapter</u> of the revised edition of *The Article Book*/<u>includes</u> presentation of a rule with examples, exercises, quizzes, and a comprehensive test. While the 50 <u>rules</u>/<u>are taught</u> to provide a logical framework for the text and serve as a handy reference, <u>students</u>/<u>will learn</u> through guided practice instead of memorization. *The Article Book*/<u>may serve</u> as either a supplement to any ESL/EFL core text or as a self-study tool for intermediate through advanced learners. *Fish Trek*/<u>is</u> a well-designed interactive computer game created specifically to help teach English article usage. <u>It</u>/<u>offers</u> six game levels, ten levels of difficulty, and a comprehensive practice session. <u>Feedback</u>/<u>is tailored</u> to the question and not the generic "right" or "wrong." A <u>plus</u> for teachers/<u>is</u> the test generator feature. While *Fish Trek* <u>software</u>/<u>supports</u> *The Article Book,* the <u>book</u> and the <u>software</u>/<u>can be used</u> separately.

Exercise 2.60 (page 64)

1. guest – IO, note – DO
2. James –IO, the instructions – DO, banana bread – DO
3. gifts – DO
4. you – DO, contribution – DO
5. computer – DO, him – IO, one – DO
6. "The Godfather" – DO
7. sand castles – DO
8. novels – DO, them – DO
9. granddaughter – IO, stories – DO
10. anniversary – DO, them – IO, trip – DO

Exercise 2.61 (page 65)

1. broke – VT, felt – VI
2. climb – VT, think – VI
3. cancelled – VT, complained – VI, gave – VT
4. prepares – VT
5. received – VT, contained – VT
6. received – VT, consisted – VI
7. walked – VI, knew – VT, was – VI, resembled – VT
8. happened – VI, travel – VI, spent – VT
9. brought – VT
10. occurs – VI, perform – VI, fall – VI

Exercise 2.62 (page 66)

1. VI
2. VI
3. VT
4. VI
5. VI
6. VI
7. VI
8. VT
9. VT
10. VI
11. VT
12. VT
13. VI
14. VT
15. VT
16. VI
17. VT
18. VT
19. VT
20. VI
21. VT
22. VI
23. VI
24. VT
25. VI

Exercise 2.63 (page 67)

1. My brother likes to <u>listen (to) good</u> music. (4)
2. I have always <u>depended ~~at~~ (on)</u> my family to take care of me. (3)
3. Many people <u>enjoyed ~~at~~ the party</u> Maria had at her house. (2)
4. Maria went shopping for shoes and <u>bought (them) in the mall</u>. (1)
5. I look <u>forward (to) going</u> to my friend's birthday party. (4)
6. She <u>waited ~~to~~ (for) him</u> for a long time, but he never came. (3)
7. Something bad <u>happened (to) my car</u> last week. I was very upset. (4)
8. Where did you <u>put it</u>? (1)
9. John was waiting for the letter and <u>finally received (it).</u> (1)
10. The class read *Great Expectations* and <u>discussed ~~about~~ it</u>. (2)
11. I got really surprised <u>~~with~~ (by)</u> his extraordinary voice. (3)
12. Josh Groban can make an impression <u>~~to~~ (on)</u> everyone who listens to his songs. (3)
13. I think he is a good singer, and I am so impressed <u>~~about~~ (with)</u> his voice. (3)
14. They could not come back home safely because good luck did not come (to) them all the time. (4)

Exercise 2.64 (page 68)

1. VT
2. VI
3. VT
4. VI
5. VI
6. VT

Exercise 2.65 (page 69)

1. 3
2. 2
3. 1
4. 3
5. 2

Exercise 2.66 (page 69)
(*Managing Readers* explores the fascinating interchange between text and margin, authorship and readership in early modern England)(IC). (William W. E. Slights considers overlooked evidence of the ways)(IC) (that early modern readers were instructed to process information, to contest opinions, and to make themselves into fully responsive consumers of texts)(DC). (The recent revolution in the protocols of reading [that was brought on by computer technology](DC) has forced questions about the nature of book-based knowledge in our global culture)(IC). (*Managing Readers* traces changes in the protocols of annotation and directed reading from medieval religious manuscripts and Renaissance handbooks for explorers, rhetoricians, and politicians to the elegant clear-text editions of the Enlightenment and the hypertexts of our own time)(IC). (The book contains twenty-two illustrations of pages from rare-book archives)(IC) (that immediately clarify the distinctive management of the reading experience during the first century-and-a-half of printing in England)(DC).

Exercise 2.67 (page 70)
Part A.

1. (Although)*Much Labouring* by Holdeman will particularly interest students of modernism

2. (While)its principal appeal will be to students of Oscar Wilde and the Victorian fin-de-siècle

3. (because)that place reminded him of the day he proposed to his wife

4. (if)I had not become a teacher, (when)I was sixteen

5. (whereas)he prefers sturdier family models, (when) they talk about cars

Exercise 2.68 (page 70)

1. (that)cannot be bought, (that)we pay for

2. (that)gathers together articles, interviews, and book reviews

3. (that)reinforce the vocabulary and idiomatic expressions

4. (that)conforms to grading criteria

5. (who)are able to concentrate, students can practice

Exercise 2.69 (page 71)

1. (That)living in New York is not going to be cheap

2. (how)marginal and decorative elements of the printed book affect interpretation

3. (that)his father was hospitalized with a heart attack, (that)he would be able to see his father alive

4. (which)exit I should take off the highway

5. (whether)he was right or wrong, (what)happened to him

Exercise 2.70 (page 72)

1. 1
2. 3
3. 3
4. 1
5. 3
6. 2
7. 3
8. 3
9. 3
10. 2
11. 2
12. 1
13. 3
14. 3
15. 3
16. 3
17. 1
18. 3
19. 2
20. 1

Exercise 2.71 (page 73)

1. 3
2. 1
3. 2
4. 4
5. 3
6. 4
7. 3
8. 4
9. 2
10. 1
11. 1
12. 2

13. 2
14. 1
15. 4
16. 3
17. 4
18. 2
19. 1
20. 3

Exercise 2.72 (page 74)

1. is
2. seem
3. has
4. is
5. were
6. is
7. lives, happens, do not
8. is
9. is
10. was
11. decides
12. were
13. was
14. were

Exercise 2.73 (page 75)

1. RO—China, and
2. CS—cars. Others
3. CS—lives. I
4. RO—pick. I
5. CS—time. Finally,
6. F—Christmas, I was ready for my trip.
7. RO—harm. They
8. CS—before, but she
9. F—plausible, many
10. F—It is very

Exercise 2.74 (page 76)

1. (F) Even though he was an experienced politician running for President and had some great ideas to improve the country's health care system, he lost.
2. (CS) The mess that the children created in their room was not easy to clean up, *so* I gave up after an hour. (OR: cleanup. I gave up)
3. (CS) The skater started the program slowly. Then she started landing difficult jumps, and (OR: so) the audience gave her a standing ovation at the end of her performance.
4. (CS) There is no doubt that Prohibition was necessary at the time, *but* it was not very popular among alcohol producers.
5. (F) If I had known that that meeting was going to be the last time that I would ever see her, *I would have* . . . (answers will vary).
6. (F) Some of the students wanting to travel to France in the summer and spend a month living with host-families and learning the language *will* . . . (answers will vary).
7. (RO) It is amazing how many people sell things online these days; some make it their daily jobs. (OR: days. Some)

 8. (RO) *Since my* sister decided to change a career after working as a business analyst for more than ten years, the family is 100 percent behind her decision.

 9. (F) Troubled by rising gas prices and concerned about the instability of the global economy, *people are . . .* (answers will vary).

10. (CS) The Browns decided to redecorate their home office. Jeannette cleaned the carpet and chose the paint, *and* Rob painted the wall.

11. (CS) This next section of the movie has a lot of interesting details and information necessary for the understanding of the plot, *so* watch it carefully.

12. (CS) Organic food is becoming very popular. Many people are willing to spend a bit more on it even though the benefits of eating organic produce have not been fully researched yet.

13. (RO) Thank you for inviting me over for dinner Saturday night; however, I am unable to make it as it also happens to be my sister's birthday that day. (OR: night. However, I)

14. (CS) My friend has been importing medical equipment; in fact, he imports three million dollars worth of equipment every quarter. (OR: equipment. In fact, he)

15. (F) Practicing tirelessly her answers to the sample interview questions and adding final touches to her resume, *she . . .* (answers will vary).

Exercise 2.75 (page 77)

 1. call, calling, called, called
 2. speak, speaking, spoke, spoken
 3. delay, delaying, delayed, delayed
 4. take, taking, took, taken
 5. go, going, went, gone
 6. fly, flying, flew, flown
 7. put, putting, put, put
 8. cry, crying, cried, cried
 9. eat, eating, ate, eaten
10. cut, cutting, cut, cut
11. visit, visiting, visited, visited
12. cringe, cringing, cringed, cringed
13. have, having, had, had
14. wear, wearing, wore, worn
15. open, opening, opened, opened

Exercise 2.76 (page 78)

The following should have a check mark:

 1. past, past participle
 2. simple
 3. past, past participle
 4. present participle
 5. simple, past, past participle
 6. past participle
 7. simple, past participle
 8. present participle
 9. past, past participle
10. simple, past, past participle
11. past
12. past, past participle

Exercise 2.77 (page 79)

take—take, takes; do not take, does not take; do . . . take, does . . . take; be   am, are, is; am not, are not, is not; am . . . , are . . . , is . . .

Exercise 2.78 (page 79)

work—worked, worked; did not work, did not work; did . . . work; did . . . work; take—took, took; did not take, did not take; did . . . take, did . . . take

Exercise 2.79 (page 79)

go—will go, will go; will not go, will not go; will . . . go, will . . . go

Exercise 2.80 (page 79)

work—am working, are working, is working; am not working, are not working, is not working; am . . . working, are . . . working, is . . . working; put—am putting, are putting, is putting; am not putting, are not putting, is not putting; am . . . putting, are . . . putting, is . . . putting

Exercise 2.81 (page 80)

open—was opening, were opening, was opening; was not opening, were not opening, was not opening; was . . . opening, were . . . opening, was . . . opening; begin—was beginning, were beginning, was beginning; was not beginning, were not beginning, was not beginning; was . . . beginning, were . . . beginning, was . . . beginning

Exercise 2.82 (page 80)

take—will be taking, will be taking; will not be taking, will not be taking; will . . . be taking, will . . . be taking; wait—will be waiting, will be waiting; will not be waiting, will not be waiting; will . . . be waiting, will . . . be waiting

Exercise 2.83 (page 80)

work—have worked, has worked; have not worked, has not worked; have . . . worked, has . . . worked; be—have been, has been; have not been, has not been; have . . . been, has . . . been

Exercise 2.84 (page 81)

work—had worked, had worked; had not worked, had not worked; had . . . worked, had . . . worked; have—had had, had had; had not had, had not had; had . . . had, had . . . had

Exercise 2.85 (page 81)

work—will have worked, will have worked; will not have worked, will not have worked; will . . . have worked, will . . . have worked; go—will have gone, will have gone; will not have gone, will not have gone; will . . . have gone, will . . . have gone

Exercise 2.86 (page 81)

take—have been taking, has been taking; have not been taking, has not been taking; have . . . been taking, has . . . been taking; check—have been checking, has been checking; have not been checking, has not been checking; have . . . been checking, has . . . been checking

Exercise 2.87 (page 82)

take—had been taking, had been taking; had not been taking, had not been taking; had . . . been taking, had . . . been taking; do—had been doing, had been doing; had not been doing, had not been doing; had . . . been doing, had . . . been doing

Exercise 2.88 (page 82)

take—will have been taking, will have been taking; will not have been taking, will not have been taking; will . . . have been taking, will . . . have been taking; work—will have been working, will have been working; will not have been working, will not have been working; will . . . have been working, will . . . have been working

Exercise 2.89 (page 83)

1. c
2. e
3. l
4. h
5. j
6. f
7. a
8. b
9. k
10. g
11. d
12. i

Exercise 2.90 (page 84)

1. choose(s)
2. recycle(s)
3. chose
4. recycled
5. will choose
6. will recyle
7. am/is/are choosing
8. am/is/are recycling
9. was/were choosing
10. was/were recycling
11. will be choosing
12. will be recycling

13. has/have chosen
14. has/have recycled
15. had chosen
16. had recycled
17. will have chosen
18. will have recycled
19. has/have been choosing
20. has/have been recycling
21. had been choosing
22. had been recycling
23. will have been choosing
24. will have been recycling

Exercise 2.91 (page 85)
The following should have a check mark: 1, 2, 5, 6, 8, 9, 11, 13, 15, 16, 19, 21, 22, 28, 31, 32, 34, 35, 36, 38, 41, 42, 44, 45, 46, 47, 48

Exercise 2.92 (page 86)
The following should have a check mark: 3, 5, 7, 8, 10, 14, 19, 22, 23, 24, 25, 26, 27, 32, 33, 34, 35, 38, 39, 40, 42, 44, 46, 47, 48

Exercise 2.93 (page 87)
Answers will vary.

Exercise 2.94 (pages 88–90)
Answers will vary according to how you count certain verb forms. For example, if you do not count modals (except *will* for future) or commands such as *Let's see* or *Show that*, then your total number of (conjugated) verbs would be 104, and your answers might look like these:

	Simple	**Progressive**	**Perfect**	**Perfect Progressive**	**TOTALS**
Present	90 = 87%	4 = 4%	0 = 0%	0 = 0%	94 = 90%
Past	8 = 8%	1 = 1%	0 = 0%	0 = 0%	9 = 9%
Future	1 = 1%	0 = 0%	0 = 0%	0 = 0%	1 = 1%
TOTALS	99 = 95%	5 = 5%	0 = 0%	0 = 0%	104 = 100%

S1: All right, is [PRES] the Moebius transformation stuff in here or is [PRES] it in the, Stahl, or is [PRES] it not in anything?

S2: Um, I don't know [PRES] I shoulda brought my notebook.

S1: I don't see [PRES] Moebius in here . . .

S3: Is [PRES] that the handout?

S1: Yeah, this was [PAST] that co—this was [PAST] conjugacy so, it might not have anything to do with Moebius.

S3: Okay.

S2: I think [PRES] it must be in Stahl like on around page one-fifty-nine, 'cuz that's [PRES] what our exercises are [PRES] out of.

S3: Does she spell [PRES] Moebius wrong? She spells [PRES] it M O B I U S.

S1: Well, no, she puts [PRES] [S2: Yeah] M O with the two, dots above it.

S2: With the two dots just like she does [PRES] in the book.

S1: I think [PRES] she spells [PRES] it right [S2: Yeah] like let me just point to where (he's) [PRES] wrong.

S2: It's [PRES] like Moebius. I can't say it like she can. She's [PRES] like Moebius.

S3: You know [PRES], I have [PRES] like this other teacher in, four-fifty, and she was [PAST] spelled [PAST] it like, M O E B I U S.

S2: That's [PRES] how they spell [PRES] it in the book.

S3: I know [PRES]. But, in our other class like four-thirty-three, spelled [PAST] it like, Natasha. So I don't know [PRES] what's [PRES] right.

S1: All right, so . . .

S2: I think [PRES], O E is [PRES] a linguistic form it's [PRES] a vowel, and it goes [PRES] like /oe/ it goes [PRES] however she says [PRES] Moebius, it goes [PRES] like that, and it's [PRES] an actual vowel in linguistics and so i think [PRES] that's [PRES] why they spell [PRES] it like that.

S1: All right, so what's [PRES] R-hat?

S3: And so does the [S2: R-hat] O-dot-dot replace [PRES] the [S1: Is [PRES] that like] O-E or something?

S2: Yeah.

S3: Okay.

S1: Is [PRES] that like [S2: I think] [PRES] R minus infinity?

S2: I'm trying [PRES PROG] to remember if it's [PRES] R minus infinity or R minus zero or . . .

S1: Or R no maybe it's [PRES] R union with infinity.

S2: Plus infinity yeah because C-hat is [PRES], the complex numbers union infinity.

S1: Right, so that must be what it is [PRES]. Okay?

S2: Allright so, show that, given any three points X Y and Z in R-hat, there is [PRES] a Moebius transformation which sends [PRES] the points zero one and infinity to X Y and Z respectively.

S1: Okay so, we wanna [PRES] find a . . . Moebius transformation . . . <PAUSE:10> zero to, minus one to Y infinity to Z.

S2: So don't we do [PRES] it like she was doing [PAST PROG] 'em in class?

S3: Was [PAST] this on Friday or, when?

S2: Um, I don't know [PRES] she just seemed [PAST] to do something like this, one we want [PRES] to go to Y, and infinity we want [PRES] to go to Z. So then we have [PRES] to write 'em, F-of-Z equals [PRES] equals [PRES] F-of-X, right isn't [PRES] that what we do [PRES]? F-of-X equals [PRES] and now we want [PRES] it to be, zero, A plus zero all over, zero, B plus zero?

S1: So we're [PRES] n—there's [PRES] no complex numbers in this so that's [PRES] kinda weird. 'Cuz the Moebius, I thought [PAST], okay well Z doesn't have [PRES] to be a complex number it can be a real number cuz real numbers are [PRES] complex numbers? [S3: yeah] Okay. [S2: yeah] All right.

S2: So, F-of-X equals [PRES], actually we only need [PRES] A to be zero right? Doesn't matter [PRES] [S1: So, you want [PRES]] what everything else is [PRES].

S1: So you want [PRES] F of-zero to equal X. Is [PRES] that what we're saying [PRES PROG]? Equal [PRES] X.

S2: Um, oops yeah.

S1: Right. So, it doesn't matter [PRES] what A is [PRES] right? And it doesn't matter [PRES] what C is [PRES]. It just mat—[PRES] and D can't equal zero. Right?

S2: Well, we have [PRES] to have, one of 'em be X.

S1: Oh right.

S3: So.

S2: So, we want [PRES] A to be one right? So it'll be [FUT] one-X, so we want [PRES] [S3: Yeah, that's [PRES]] A to equal one, B to equal zero, C to equal zero and D [S3: B to equal zero, C to equal zero, and D] to equal one.

S1: Oh, but here's [PRES], here's [PRES] what the p—but we're [PRES] supposed to, we're mapping [PRES PROG] zero to X so isn't [PRES], you stick [PRES] zero in for Z right? [S2: Uhuh] not X. [S2: Right.] So you wanna [PRES] make, you wanna [PRES] make [S3: You wanna [PRES] make] B X. You know [PRES] what I'm saying [PRES PROG]?

Exercise 2.95 (pages 91–92)

Answers will vary according to how you count certain verb forms. For example, if you do not count modals (except *will* for future) or commands such as *Just stay here*, then your total number of (conjugated) verbs would be 77, and your answers might look like these:

	Simple	**Progressive**	**Perfect**	**Perfect Progressive**	**TOTALS**
Present	5 = 7%	0 = 0%	3 = 4%	0 = 0%	8 = 11%
Past	58 = 75%	4 = 5%	7 = 9%	0 = 0%	69 = 89%
Future	0 = 0%	0 = 0%	0 = 0%	0 = 0%	0 = 0%
TOTALS	63 = 82%	4 = 5%	10 = 13%	0 = 0%	77 = 100%

Hurricane Camille struck [PAST] the coast of southern Mississippi hard on the evening of August 17, 1969, killing 259 people in its wake. A handful of remarkable survival tales emerged [PAST], including that of 33-year old Mary Ann Gerlach, who gained [PAST] near-instant national fame with her astonishing survival story. She and her sixth husband, Frederick (or "Fritz," as most people knew [PAST] him), had lived [PAST PERF] at the Richelieu Apartments. Both had worked [PAST PERF] night shifts the evening before the hurricane, she as a waitress and he as a Seabee in the Navy. Mary Ann told [PAST] reporters:

> The first thing that popped [PAST] into my mind was [PAST] party time! We all got [PAST] together and decided [PAST] we were going [PAST PROG] to have a hurricane party on the third floor. I went [PAST] out and got [PAST] all kinds of stuff to fix, you know [PRES], sandwiches and hors d'oeuvres. Well, all the Civil Defense people had come [PAST PERF] up trying to get us out, and the manager and his wife kept [PAST] telling us, "There's [PRES] no need to go. It's [PRES] ridiculous, so just stay here."

Mary Ann and Fritz never did join [PAST] the group on the third floor. They decided [PAST] to nap first, but thumping sounds from below awakened [PAST] them around 10:00 PM. The electricity was [PAST] out by then, and they ventured [PAST] into the living room by flashlight. To their horror, the Gulf of Mexico was [PAST] one-third of the way up their second-story picture window, some twenty feet above normal sea level. As they dashed [PAST] back to their bedroom, the front window imploded [PAST], the sea rushed [PAST] in, and the building shuddered [PAST]. Their only option now was [PAST] to get ready to swim. Unfortunately, years earlier as a new enlistee, Fritz had talked [PAST PERF] a buddy into passing his swimming test for him, and now that ruse came [PAST] back to haunt him since he didn't know [PAST] how to swim at all. With waist-deep water swirling around them and their furniture floating, Mary Ann blew [PAST] up an air mattress that she kept [PAST] for the swimming pool and gave [PAST] it to Fritz.

Moments later, the rear window shattered [PAST] and she swam [PAST] out with the current—smack into a maze of electrical wires. The sea, surging in through the front and out the rear of the apartment, swept [PAST] Fritz out behind her. She disentangled [PAST] herself and pushed [PAST] off from the doomed building. "My legs," she explained [PAST], "were [PAST] real strong, you know [PRES], from doing waitress work for so long." Meanwhile, Fritz drowned [PAST]. Several days later, his body was found [PAST] tangled in a tree several miles inland.

Some six hours later, unable to walk and wearing only tattered shorts and the ragged remnants of a short-sleeved sweatshirt, Mary Ann sat [PAST] shivering in the mud into the morning. She spied [PAST] a man tramping through the debris and called [PAST] to him for help. He asked [PAST] if she had seen [PAST PERF] his wife. "No, I haven't seen [PRES PERF] anyone alive but you," she replied [PAST]. The man stumbled [PAST] away in a trance, repeating his wife's name over and over.

She huddled [PAST], still shivering, for more than an hour before the next person came [PAST] along, a young man she recognized [PAST] as a local post office clerk. She called [PAST] out to him. The postal clerk and the two other men carried [PAST] Mary Ann to a high school, where school officials were converting [PAST PROG] one area of the school to a temporary morgue and most of the rest of the building was sheltering [PAST PROG] survivors. A few hours later, several National Guard troops transferred [PAST] her to the Miramar Nursing Home. There, as her wounds were being [PAST PROG] tended, Mary Ann explained [PAST] to the nurses that she was [PAST] the sole survivor of the Richelieu Apartments.

The word quickly got [PAST] out to the reporters, and as journalists swarmed [PAST] in to interview her over and again, Mary Ann got [PAST] better and better at remembering various details of her extraordinary survival story. Nationwide, hundreds of broadcasts and newspapers reported [PAST] that Mary Ann Gerlach had been [PAST PERF] the sole survivor out of two dozen revelers at a "hurricane party" in the ill-fated apartment building.

In truth, at least eight others had survived [PAST PERF] the destruction of the Richelieu. Several of them had [PAST] heroic motives for remaining there that terrible night, and all suffered [PAST] consequences as agonizing as Mary Ann's harrowing experience. Camille's "hurricane party," however, has become [PRES PERF] embedded in American folklore, and perhaps some good has come [PRES PERF] from that. Wittingly or not, Mary Ann Gerlach raised [PAST] the consciousness of millions of Americans that hurricanes are [PRES] not auspicious occasions for partying.

Exercise 2.96 (page 93)
Answers will vary.

Chapter 3 (pages 94–200)

ELL Grammar Key 1: to be

Exercise 3.1.1 (page 94)
be; am, is, are; was, were; being; been

3.1.2 (page 95)
a. 4
b. 1
c. 3
d. 2
e. 2

f. 4
g. 2
h. 3

3.1.3 (page 95)
is and *was* end in *–s; are* and *were* end in *-re*

3.1.4 (page 95)
Put *not* after the form of *be*

3.1.5 (page 96)
Be contractions are possible in both affirmative and negative in the present tense but only in the negative in the past tense.

3.1.6 (page 96)
Contractions are considered less formal and occur much more in spoken language than in written language. Contractions can (potentially) make a speaker sound more friendly.

3.1.7 (page 96)
Simply move the form of *be* to in front of the subject, thereby inverting the subject and the verb. Thus, the formula is *be* + SUBJECT.

3.1.8 (page 96)
Invert the subject and the form of *be*. Substitute the correct question word (e.g., *what* or *where*) for the actual answer and place it at the beginning of the question. Thus, the formula is *wh-word* + *be* + SUBJECT.

3.1.9 (page 97)
This is a map of North America. The country to the north of the United States <u>is</u> Canada. Canada <u>is</u> a very large country, but not so many people live in Canada. The population <u>is</u> 29,000,000. The leaders in Canada want more people to come to live in their country. I think they <u>are</u> right because Canada needs more people.

Canada has two official languages. These two languages <u>are</u> English and French. Most of the people who speak French live in Quebec. Quebec <u>is</u> a large province in Canada. The capital of Canada is Ottawa. The largest cities <u>are</u> Toronto, Vancouver, and Montreal. Vancouver is in the west, but Toronto and Montreal <u>are</u> not in the west. Montreal is in the eastern part of the country, and Toronto is in the central part of Canada.

Action Research (page 97): Answers will vary.

ELL Grammar Key 2: *Verb Tenses to Express Present Time*

Exercise 3.2.1 (page 98)
Many examples are possible, so answers will vary. A common example is using simple present tense for a future time, as in *The president's plane arrives in ten minutes.* Another common example is using present progressive tense for future time, as in *We're having dinner with your parents tomorrow night.*

3.2.2 (page 98)
Answers will vary.

3.2.3 (page 99)
Some researchers advocate teaching present progressive tense first because that tense is much more frequent in English. The counterargument for the more traditional order with simple present first is that ELLs can learn the base form of a verb first before learning an expanded version such as present progressive tense.

3.2.4 (page 99)
take, takes

3.2.5 (page 99)
a. If a verb ends in a consonant + -*y*, then change the -*y* to -*i* and add -*es*. *studies, tries*
b. If a verb ends in a consonant + -*o*, add -*es*. *does, goes*

3.2.6 (page 99)
am taking, is taking, are taking

3.2.7 (page 99)
In a one-syllable word, double the final consonant if there is only one vowel before it. Do not double the final consonant if there is not one (and only one) vowel before it. In a two-syllable word ending in C–V–C, double the last consonant only if the second syllable is stressed.

3.2.8 (page 100)
a. 3
b. 4
c. 2
d. 3
e. 2
f. 1
g. 4
h. 2
i. 3
j. 1

3.2.9 (page 101)
has taken, have taken

3.2.10 (page 101)
Add the suffix –*ed*: *played, jumped, skated.*

3.2.11 (page 101)
The rules are the same.

3.2.12 (page 101)
Common irregular endings include -*en, -ne,* or -*n*, but there are other possibilities.

3.2.13 (page 102)
a. 2
b. 3
c. 1
d. 3
e. 1
f. 2
g. 3
h. 1

3.2.14 (page 103)
has been taking, have been taking

3.2.15 (page 103)
a. 1
b. 2
c. 2
d. 2
e. 1

3.2.16 (page 103)
do/does + not + VERB
am/is/are + not + VERB + -*ing*
has/have + not + PRESENT PARTICIPLE
has/have + not + been + VERB + -*ing*

3.2.17 (page 104)
The simple present tense. For simple present tense, a negative requires an additional auxiliary: *do/does not* + VERB. *Do not* is used with *I, you, we,* or *they*; *does not* is used with *he, she,* or *it.* The other tenses add just a negative word *not.*

3.2.18 (page 104)
a. 3
b. 1
c. 2
d. 3
e. 3
f. 1
g. 4
h. 4

3.2.19 (page 105)

Verb Tense	Affirmative	Negative
Simple Present	———	*don't*
		doesn't
Present Progressive	*I'm*	———
	he's/she's/it's	*isn't*
	you're/we're/they're	*aren't*
Present Perfect	*I've/you've/we've/they've*	*haven't*
	he's/she's/it's	*hasn't*
Present Perfect Progressive	*I've/you've/we've/they've*	*haven't*
	he's/she's/it's	*hasn't*

3.2.20 (page 105)
We can contract *has* only when it is an auxiliary verb. We cannot contract it when it is the main verb. It cannot be contracted in an affirmative short answer.

3.2.21 (page 105)
Answers will vary. Most ELLs have great difficulty with present perfect tense because it can be used to describe both finished actions and current actions. ELLs may be confused how one tense can be used for completely different meanings. ELLs find this tense difficult in both negative and affirmative.

3.2.22 (page 106)
a. 1
b. 2
c. 3
d. 4
e. 5
f. 2
g. 3
h. 2

3.2.23 (page 107)
To sum up, cell phones (have been) with us for a relatively short period of time, but they have already become an extremely important mode of communication. Over time, people (have become) more attracted to this amazing little device. The result now is that almost everyone (owns) a cell phone. In fact, some people (have) multiple cell phones. Although it is a popular way to communicate, cell phones (have) many negative impacts on people. Some people really (don't) like to use cell phones, and their reasons for avoiding them (are) very convincing. A cell phone is a disruptive instrument and often endangers people's lives. In my opinion, the negative aspects of this tiny device (outweigh) the positive aspects by a wide margin.

Action Research (page 107): Answers will vary.

ELL Grammar Key 3: *Verb Tenses to Express Past Time*

3.3.1 (page 108)
Answers will vary.

3.3.2 (page 108)
One

3.3.3 (page 109)
For verbs of one syllable that end in consonant + vowel + consonant (C-V-C), double the last consonant and then add *–ed: slip* → *slipped, hum* → *hummed, rob* → *robbed*. For verbs of two syllables that end in C-V-C, double the last consonant before adding *–ed* if the stress is on the second syllable: *commít* → *committed, refér* → *referred*. If the stress is on the first syllable, however, we do NOT double the final consonant: *ópen* → *opened, háppen* → *happened, vísit* → *visited*.

3.3.4 (page 109)
Answers will vary. Possible answers include: *was, went, got, saw, ran*

3.3.5 (page 109)
a. 3
b. 4
c. 1
d. 2
e. 2
f. 1

3.3.6 (page 110)
two: *was eating, were eating*

3.3.7 (page 110)
a. 4
b. 2
c. 2
d. 3
e. 1

3.3.8 (page 111)
two: *have worked, has worked*

3.3.9 (page 111)
Add –ed: *jumped.* Sometimes we double the last consonant as previously discussed: *begged.*

3.3.10 (page 111)
Common endings for the past participle forms of irregular verbs include *-en, -ne,* or *-n,* but there are other possibilities.

3.3.11 (page 111)
Only a small number of English verbs are irregular, and you must only memorize the irregular verbs most commonly used. In addition, there are patterns even within the irregular verbs. For example, many one-syllable words ending in *–t* do not change: *cut, cut, cut* and *let, let, let.*

3.3.12 (page 112)
Answers will vary.

3.3.13 (page 113)
a. 4
b. 4
c. 5
d. 3
e. 2
f. 1
g. 5
h. 4

3.3.14 (page 114)
one: *had worked*

3.3.15 (page 114)
a. 1
b. 2
c. 1
d. 2
e. 2

3.3.16 (page 115)
one: *had been working*

3.3.17 (page 115)
a. 1
b. 2
c. 1
d. 1

3.3.18 (page 115)
one: *used to work*

3.3.19 (page 115)
one: *would work*

3.3.20 (page 115)
They share the idea that a past action happened repeatedly, but it is no longer (usually) done now. *When I was a teenager, my dad and I <u>used to/would</u> go fishing almost every weekend.*

3.3.21 (page 116)
Used to can introduce a past fact or state of being that is no longer true. *When I was a teenager, my family <u>used to</u> live in Mexico.*

3.3.22 (page 116)
a. 2
b. 2
c. 1
d. 2
e. 1

3.3.23 (page 117)
did + not + VERB
was/were + not + VERB *+ -ing*
has/have + not + PAST PARTICIPLE
had + not + PAST PARTICIPLE
had + not + been + VERB *+ -ing*
did + not + use to + VERB
would + not + VERB

3.3.24 (page 117)

Simple past tense. In simple past tense, a negative takes the form: *did not* + VERB. ELLs have a difficult time with adding an auxiliary and removing *–ed* from the verb.

3.3.25 (page 117)

1. omission of *did*
2. use of *be*
3. including *–ed*

3.3.26 (page 118)

a. 5
b. 7
c. 1
d. 5
e. 4
f. 3
g. 6
h. 2

3.3.27 (page 119)

Verb Tense/ Expression	Affirmative	Negative
Simple Past	—	*didn't*
Present Perfect	*I've/you've/we've/they've*	*haven't*
	he's/she's/it's	*hasn't*
Past Perfect	*I'd/you'd/he'd/she'd/it'd/we'd/they'd*	*hadn't*
Past Perfect Progressive	*I'd/you'd/he'd/she'd/it'd/we'd/they'd*	*hadn't*
Used to	—	*didn't*
Would	*I'd/you'd/he'd/she'd/it'd/we'd/they'd*	*wouldn't*

3.3.28 (page 119)

did + subject + VERB
invert *was/were* before the subject
invert *has/have* before the subject
invert *had* before the subject
invert *had* before the subject + VERB *–ing*
did + subject + *use to* + VERB
invert *would* before the subject

3.3.29 (page 120)

a. 4
b. 6
c. 1
d. 2
e. 3
f. 5

3.3.30 (page 121)

The event that I will never forget is the day when a snake **was** really close to me. I remember that it was a Tuesday because that is the day that garbage is collected in my neighborhood. I was walking outside with a big bag of trash and was thinking about all the other things that I had to do that day. I **had** just set the garbage bag down on the curb when I **heard** an unusual sound. It was a very slow and steady hissing sound. I **was** so nervous. I was confused because I **did** not know what to do. My first reaction was to turn and run, but I did not know if making a sudden movement was a good idea or not. After two or three seconds of listening to that hissing, I **decided** to run away as fast as I could. When I was about thirty feet away, I looked back. However, by the time I looked back, the snake **had** already started its escape. I saw the snake writhing away. I am glad that I **did** not see the snake when it was near me.

Action Research (page 121): Answers will vary.

ELL Grammar Key 4: *Verb Tenses to Express Future Time*

3.4.1 (page 122)
We rarely use this future tense.

3.4.2 (page 122)
Answers will vary.

3.4.3 (page 122)
We use *be going to* in order to talk about future actions or events that we have already planned.

3.4.4 (page 123)
three: *am going to take, is going to take, are going to take*

3.4.5 (page 123)
a. 3
b. 1
c. 1
d. 2
e. 3

3.4.6 (page 123)
an unplanned future action, a request to do something

3.4.7 (page 123)
one: *will take*

3.4.8 (page 124)
a. 3
b. 2
c. 1
d. 1
e. 2
f. 3

3.4.9 (page 124)
three: *am taking, is taking, are taking*

3.4.10 (page 125)
a. 2
b. 1
c. 1
d. 2

3.4.11 (page 125)
Answers will vary.

3.4.12 (page 125)
We sometimes use *will* in a dependent clause (after *if*) to indicate acceptance of a task, as in *If you will help me with this letter, I will pay you $50.*

3.4.13 (page 126)
a. 2
b. 2
c. 1
d. 2
e. 1

3.4.14 (page 127)
one: *will be taking*

3.4.15 (page 127)
a. 1
b. 2
c. 2
d. 1

3.4.16 (page 128)
one: *will have taken*

3.4.17 (page 128)
a. 1
b. 2
c. 2
d. 1

3.4.18 (page 129)
one: *will have been taking*

3.4.19 (page 129)
a. 2
b. 1
c. 2
d. 1

3.4.20 (page 130)
How do you form the negative of these verb tenses?

Tense/Expression	Negative Forms
be going to	*I am + not + going to* + VERB *you/we/they are + not + going to* + VERB *he/she/it + is + not + going to* + VERB
Present Progressive	*I am + not + going to* + VERB *you/we/they are + not* + VERB + *–ing* *he/she/it + is + not* + VERB + *–ing*
Simple Present	*I/you/we/they + do + not* + VERB *he/she/it + does + not* + VERB
Simple Future	*I/you/he/she/it/we/they + will + not* + VERB
Future Progressive	*I/you/he/she/it/we/they + will + not + be* + VERB + *–ing*
Future Perfect	*I/you/he/she/it/we/they + will + not + have* + PAST PARTICIPLE
Future Perfect Progressive	*I/you/he/she/it/we/they + will + not + have + been* + VERB + *–ing*

3.4.21 (page 130)
Answers will vary. One possibility is the apparently simple word *will*. ELLs routinely attempt to insert some auxiliary such as *do* (*I don't will go*) or *does* (*She does will sing*).

3.4.22 (page 131)
a. 1. According to the most recent weather report, severe weather IS not going to hit our area until tomorrow morning. Everyone should be prepared for these storms.
b. 2. Unfortunately, Joshua' parents WILL NOT attend his graduation ceremony.
c. 1. Does your family need a vacation? Surely your family IS not going to wait any longer to make plans for your family's fun trip, right?
d. 2. I think our professor WILL NOT give a quiz tomorrow.
e. 1. Now that Ohio has increased the amount of early voting time, voters in that midwestern state ARE not going to experience the long voting lines that they did on the last election day.

3.4.23 (page 132)
Complete this chart with the possible contractions.

Verb Tense/ Expression	Affirmative	Negative
be going to; Present Progressive	*I'm*	————
	he's/she's/it's	*isn't*
	you're/we're/they're	*aren't*
Simple Future; Future Progressive; Future Perfect; Future Perfect Progressive	*I'll/you'll/he'll/she'll/it'll/we'll/they'll*	*won't*
Simple Present	——————	*don't*
	——————	*doesn't*

3.4.24 (page 133)
Complete this chart with the question forms of these verb tenses.

Verb Tense/ Expression	Question Form
Simple Present	*do + I/you/we/they + VERB* *does + he/she/it + VERB*
Be going to	*am + I + going to + VERB + –ing* *are + you/we/they + going to + VERB + –ing* *is + he/she/it + going to + VERB + –ing*
Present Progressive	*am + I + VERB + –ing* *are + you/we/they + VERB + –ing* *is + he/she/it + VERB + –ing*
Simple Future	*will + I/you/he/she/it/we/they + VERB*
Future Progressive	*will + I/you/he/she/it/we/they + be + VERB + –ing*
Future Perfect	*will + I/you/he/she/it/we/they + have + Past Participle*
Future Perfect Progressive	*will + I/you/he/she/it/we/they + have + been + Present Participle*

3.4.25 (page 134)
a. 2   b. 1   c. 1   d. 2   e. 2

3.4.26 (page 135)
Every summer Jim and I take a trip, and this summer is no exception. In fact, our trip this summer may end up being our best ever because we <u>are going</u> to Italy. We have been looking forward to this trip to Italy for a long time, and next week we <u>are going to fly</u> there. Finally, our trip is going to <u>happen</u>. We have a great guidebook and will continue looking at information on as many websites as possible right up until the day we <u>leave</u>. We don't know many specific details about the places we'll <u>be visiting</u> (or <u>visit</u>), but by the time our flight <u>leaves</u> here, we <u>will have read</u> a lot and be much better prepared to see Italy. When our flight <u>takes off</u>, I know that both of us will be so happy that our dream to see Rome and Florence will finally become a reality.

Action Research (page 135): Answers will vary.

ELL Grammar Key 5: *Count and Non-Count Nouns*

3.5.1 (page 136)
A noun that names something you can count.

3.5.2 (page 136)
Answers will vary.

3.5.3 (page 136)
Answers will vary.

3.5.4 (page 136)
Sentence 2. The reason is that when a descriptive adjective (i.e., *designer*) separates the determiner and the noun, ELLs often omit the article.

3.5.5 (page 136)
Answers will vary, but possible answers include *have dinner, in school, on vacation, at home, at work, by phone*

3.5.6 (page 137)
A noun that cannot be counted.

3.5.7 (page 137)
Answers will vary.

3.5.8 (page 137)
Answers will vary.

3.5.9 (page 137)
Anwers will vary.

3.5.10 (page 137)
A piece of luggage. ELLs often associate *piece* with something that is broken or separated.

3.5.11 (page 138)
We use *how many* with plural count nouns. We use *how much* with non-count nouns.

3.5.12 (page 138)
When in doubt, it is always correct to use *a lot of* with both count and non-count nouns. If we are not naming the noun, we omit the preposition *of.*

3.5.13 (page 138)
We use *a few* with plural count nouns. We use *a little* with non-count nouns.

3.5.14 (page 138)
I have a little watch refers to the size of the watch because *watch* is a count noun. *I have a little time* refers to the amount of time the person has because *time* here is a non-count noun.

3.5.15 (page 138)
I have a little money has a positive connotation. *I have little money* has a negative connotation. This is an advanced-level grammar point.

3.5.16 (page 139)
a great deal of, a large number of, numerous

3.5.17 (page 139)
a. 1
b. 2
c. 1
d. 5
e. 3
f. 3
g. 5
h. 3
i. 4
j. 1
k. 3
l. 3

3.5.18 (page 140)

Do you have good credit? Do you remember when you applied for your first credit card? Have you ever been declined for a credit card from a company because of your credit history? Well, if you have had that experience, you know what a credit card is. According to the msnmoney.com website, many Americans carry between five to ten credit cards. Other people carry up to 50, which is really a lot. As we all know, having too many credit cards has a negative effect on your (OR: a) credit report.

Action Research (page 140): Answers will vary.

ELL Grammar Key 6: *Prepositions*

3.6.1 (page 141)
A word that shows the relationship between a noun (or pronoun) and the rest of the words in the sentence, often giving us information about place, time, and direction.

3.6.2 (page 141)
Answers will vary. Possible answers include *after, at, beneath, for, from, in, of, on, off, over, to, under.*

3.6.3 (page 141)
a. 1
b. 1
c. 4
d. 3
e. 2

3.6.4 (page 141)
Answers will vary. Possible answers include *on cloud nine, beyond a shadow of a doubt, from head to toe, in trouble.*

3.6.5 (page 142)
The combination of a preposition and its object (and any modifiers such as articles or adjectives).

3.6.6 (page 142)

Place	Time	Direction
in the park	by noon	to the bus station
behind the house	at 3 PM	from school
on an island	around 7 PM	toward the light
next to the tree	on October 7th	into the forest

3.6.7 (page 142)
a. prep + article + obj
b. prep + obj
c. prep + article + adj + obj
d. prep + obj
e. prep + article + obj

3.6.8 (page 143)
Answers will vary. Possible answers include:
two words: in January (prep + obj)
three words: in the morning (prep + article + obj)
four words: in the early morning (prep + article + adj + obj)

3.6.9 (page 143)
a. We generally put the place phrase before the time phrase. Examples will vary, but one example is: *Please put your shoes in the suitcase before dinner.*
   Example answers will vary.
b. We generally arrange the phrases from smaller to larger: *The book is in the box on the table. Our meeting was at 3 PM on Monday.*
   Example answers will vary.

3.6.10 (page 144)

Answers will vary. Possible answers include *without, within, with, upon, up, until, under, toward.*

3.6.11 (page 144)

Answers will vary. Possible answers include: *according to, ahead of, as for, because of, close to, due to, far from, instead of*

3.6.12 (page 144)

Answers will vary. Possible answers include: *in addition to, in back of, in case of, on top of.*

3.6.13 (page 144)

Answers will vary but should be based on the pyramid on page 167 in the Handbook.

3.6.14 (page 144)

We use *for* with a period of time: *I've worked here for ten years.*
We use *since* with the name of the start time: *I've worked here since 2000.*

3.6.15 (page 145)

When talking about the past, we use *before* with the name of a specific point of time: *The game is before Monday.*
When talking about the past, we use *ago* with the name of a period of time: *My parents called me two days ago.*

3.6.16 (page 145)

When talking about the future, we use *in* with a general period of time: *The new cars will be available in two weeks.*
When talking about the future, we use *after* with the name of a period of time: *The car will be ready after Tuesday.*

3.6.17 (page 145)

We use *for* with a general period of time. We use *for* to answer the question *How long? They visited France for two weeks.*
We use *during* with the name of a period of time. We use *during* to answer the question *When? They went to the Louvre during their trip.*

3.6.18 (page 145)

Generally, we do not use a preposition after *enter*. The verb *go* must be followed by the preposition *to* (or *in*).

3.6.19 (page 145)

Rote memorization, direct teacher instruction followed by practice, and/or massive exposure through extensive reading.

   Exposure works well after direct instruction because direct instruction increases the likelihood that learners will actually notice certain features in the language, in this case preposition combinations.

3.6.20 (page 146)

to	with	of
accustomed to confusing to harmful to important to married to opposed to related to similar to	acquainted with all right with bored with disappointed with familiar with frustrated with happy with involved with okay with pleased with satisfied with	afraid of certain of composed of full of guilty of in favor of innocent of proud of sick of sure of tired of
about	**at**	**for**
angry about certain about concerned about confused about excited about happy about sorry about sure about worried about	angry at bad at good at surprised at	bad for famous for good for important for known for necessary for ready for responsible for
by	**from**	**in**
annoyed by bored by embarrassed by surprised at/by	different from divorced from far from tired from	disappointed in interested in involved in successful in

3.6.21 (page 147)
Answers will vary according to an individual's perspective, but possible answers include:

Idiom	The Contribution of the Preposition to the Idiom's Meaning
a. *to be fed up*	Medium contribution: *up* is often an intensifier; here it means that you have been given too much to do or deal with.
b. *on the dot*	Weak contribution: you might imagine someone standing on a coin.
c. *Not on your life!*	Weak contribution: There is no obvious reason to use *on* with the word *life*.
d. *over one's head*	Strong contribution: If something is *over* or more than something, it often means "too much," and the idiom *to be over one's head* means that some situation is more than you can handle.
e. *under the weather*	Medium to strong contribution: If you are under something, it implies a negative situation, and *to be under the weather* does indicate a negative situation. In addition, it might imply that the weather is in control, not the person.

3.6.22 (page 148)

a. 5
b. 1
c. 3
d. 2
e. 4
f. 3
g. 2
h. 4
i. 1
j. 5
k. 1
l. 2

3.6.23 (page 149)

a. 1
b. 3 (OR: 1)
c. 2
d. 2
e. 3 (OR: 1)
f. 1
g. 3 (OR: 1)
h. 3 (OR: 1)
i. 2
j. 2
k. 1
l. 1

3.6.24 (page 150)

Let me tell you <u>about</u> my uncle Luis. He is the most hard-working person I know. He started working <u>on</u> the family farm when he was just twelve years old. Because he worked and took care <u>of</u> the family, he never went <u>to</u> college, but he is smart <u>about</u> life. Everyone in the family has a lot respect <u>for</u> him, and all family members come to him <u>for</u> advice. He is funny and welcoming, but <u>at</u> the same time, he is always willing to help anyone in need.

Action Research (page 150): Answers will vary.

ELL Grammar Key 7: *Articles*

3.7.1 (page 151)

Indefinite articles: a, an; Definite article: the

3.7.2 (page 151)

Article usage varies considerably from language to language. Zero article in English may be confusing because the ELL's language may require an article.

3.7.3 (page 151)

a house	*a* university	*a* clock
an hour	*a* key	*a* book
a uniform	*an* apple	*an* idea

3.7.4 (page 151)

Use *a* before a noun or an adjective (+ noun) that begins with a consonant sound.
Use *an* before a noun or an adjective (+ noun) that begins with a vowel sound.
Words beginning with the letter *h* or *u* can be problematic. The use of *a* and *an* depends on the beginning sound of the next word. We say *a house* but *an hour*. We say *an umbrella* but *a university*.

3.7.5 (page 152)

Answers will vary.

3.7.6 (page 152)

In two situations you use no article: (a) when you want to talk about a category or group in general, (b) when talking about an abstract noun such as a feeling or idea.

3.7.7 (page 153)

a. *a excellent job:*   *a* should be *an* since a vowel sound follows
b. *a good advice:*   no *a/an* with non-count nouns
c. *in United States:*   countries that look plural are preceded by *the*
d. *most wonderful person:* the superlative form of an adjective is preceded by *the*
e. *Gulf of Mexico:*   most bodies of waters (except lakes) are preceded by *the*
f. *the honesty:*   abstract ideas have no article

3.7.8 (page 153)

a. 4
b. 1
c. 3
d. 2
e. 4
f. 2
g. 1
h. 2
i. 1
j. 3
k. 4
l. 3

3.7.9 (page 154)

I am originally from Sao Paolo. It is a great town with over 15 million people. ~~The~~ People in Brazil call Sao Paolo the financial capital of the country because the city has a lot of banks and businesses. It is like New York. Living in Sao Paolo may seem difficult to some. The traffic is always slow, and the pollution there is becoming a big problem, but I love my home town.

Action Research (page 154): Answers will vary.

ELL Grammar Key 8: *Pronunciation of –s and –ed*

3.8.1 (page 155)

/s/, /z/, /əz/

3.8.2 (page 155)

/t/, /d/, /əd/

3.8.3 (page 155)

Knowing the correct pronunciation of *-ed* is important because it is a difficult pronunciation point, and it is very common. The *-ed* can be used in four verb tenses (simple past, present perfect, past perfect, future perfect). (It can also be used for past participles used as adjectives: *a bored student* or *some annoyed customers*.)

3.8.4 (page 155)

c

3.8.5 (page 155)

Place, manner, voicing

3.8.6 (page 155)

Voiced sounds are made by vibration of one's vocal cords. Voiceless sounds are without the vibration.

3.8.7 (page 155)
Voiced: /d/, /g/, /l/,/o/, /n/, /i/, /ə/, /v/, /m/, /ɪ/, /r/, /z/, /a/; Voiceless: /f/, /s/, /k/, /t/, /θ/

3.8.8 (page 156)
a. decided /əd/, /t/
b. followed /d/, /əd/
c. talked /t/, /d/
d. blinked /t/, /d/
e. charged /d/, /t/

3.8.9 (page 156)
a. passengers /z/, /s/
b. cups /s/, /z/
c. ties /z/, /əz/
d. faxes, /əz/, /z/
e. toys /z/, /s/

3.8.10 (page 157)
a. Maria enjoys (V, /z/), books (N, /s/), operas (N, /z/)
b. Sam takes (V, /s/), arrives (V, /z/)
c. wears (V, /z/) glasses (N, /əz/), contacts (N, /s/)
d. snacks (N, /s/) favorites (N, /z/), apples (N, /z/), pears (N, /z/), apricots (N, /s/), bananas (N, /z/)
e. likes (V, /s/), vegetables (N, /s/), tomatoes (N, /z/), cucumbers (N, /z/), radishes (N, /əz/), potatoes (N, /z/)

3.8.11 (page 157)
Words that end in /s/, /z/, /ch/, /sh/, /ge/ are followed by /əz/. Words that end in a voiced sound (except /z/ and /ge/ are followed by /z/. Words that end in a voiceless sound (except /s/,/ch/, /sh/) are followed by /s/

3.8.12 (page 157)
Words that end in /t/ or /d/ are followed by /əd/. Words that end in a voiced sound (except /d/) are followed by /d/. Words that end in a voiceless sound (except /t/) are followed by /t/.

3.8.13 (page 157)

/t/	/d/	/əd/
faxed	disarmed	avoided
fetched	chewed	calculated
influenced	closed	guided
disliked	explained	educated
faced	imagined	extended
		guarded

3.8.14 (page 158)

/s/	/z/	/əz/
cats	bees	judges
plants	dogs	reaches
works	trees	houses
elephants	birds	washes
giraffes	arrives	dresses
	follows	

3.8.15 (page 158)
Answers will vary. Possible answers include *breaks:* He breaks a bottle in the room; *liked:* I liked all the students; *raised:* He raised an elephant; *plays:* She plays all day long.

3.8.16 (page 158)
You can present the words in groups and emphasize the final sounds, practice the words in phrases, or choose a song that has many /s/ or /z/ sounds. Also, have them repeat the word and notice how the vocal cords vibrate for /z/ by placing their fingers lightly on their throat as they pronounce the sounds.

3.8.17 (page 159)
Answers will vary. Possible answers include *disliked, faced, fetched, influenced, kicked, laughed, missed, watched.*

3.8.18 (page 159)
Answers will vary. Possible answers include *followed, listened, changed, chewed, plowed, explained, cried, cared.*

3.8.19 (page 159)
Answers will vary. Possible answers include *shouted, voted, trotted, guarded, avoided, calculated, saturated, plotted.*

3.8.20 (page 159)
Answers will vary. Possible answers include *presents, works, pots, cats, rabbits, plants, looks, laughs.*

3.8.21 (page 159)
Answers will vary. Possible answers include *dogs, movies, channels, pencils, trees, flowers, cars, bees.*

3.8.22 (page 159)
Answers will vary. Possible answers include *classes, houses, judges, beaches, dresses, matches, pleases, washes.*

3.8.23 (page 160)
a. [come + /z/] /m/ is voiced, so it combines with /z/
b. [give + /z/][persevere + /z/] /v/ and /r/ are voiced, so they combine with /z/
c. [needs + /z/], [Volume + /z/] /d/ and /m/ are voiced, so they combine with /z/
d. [cook + /t/] /k/ is voiceless, so it combines with /t/; [measured + /d/] /r/ is voiced, so it combines with /d/
e. [mix + /t/] /s/ is voiceless, so it combines with /t/; [key + /z/] all vowels are voiced, so they combine with /z/
f. [kid + /z/] /d/ is voiced, so it combines with /z/

3.8.24 (page 161)
[month+/s/], [week+/s/], [fail+/d/], [point+/s/], [mother+/z/], [do+/z/] [what+/s/] [day+/s/].

Action Research (page 161): Answers will vary

ELL Grammar Key 9: *Adjective Clauses and Reductions*

3.9.1 (page 162)
An adjective clause describes or gives more info about a noun. It usually begins with *who, that, which, whom, or whose.*

3.9.2 (page 162)
A typical position of an adjective clause in a sentence is immediately after the noun that it modifies.

3.9.3 (page 162)
Who, that, which, whom, or *whose* are relative pronouns. You can omit *that, which,* and *whom* when they are functioning as objects and *which* and *whom* when they do not follow a preposition at the beginning of a clause.

3.9.4 (page 162)
People: *who, whom, that.* Things: *that, which.* Both: *that*

3.9.5 (page 162)
Answers will vary. Possible answers include
a.   A man <u>who</u> builds houses is a carpenter.
b.   The news <u>that</u> is interesting to me pertains to politics.
c.   This book is a type of literature <u>which</u> is interesting to me.

3.9.6 (page 162)
Answers will vary. Possible answers include
a.   I hope to meet the person <u>whom</u> you hired.
b.   This book is the type <u>which</u> Sally likes.
c.   This car is the kind <u>that</u> Kelly likes.

3.9.7 (page 163)
Clauses in which the relative pronoun functions as the subject should be taught first because this type is easier for ELLs to work with.

3.9.8 (page 163)
A reduced adjective clause is really an adjective phrase because it does not contain a subject and a verb. It has been reduced to a present participle, a past participle, or a prepositional phrase.

3.9.9 (page 163)
Answers will vary. Possible answers include
a.   People <u>living on the beach</u> can watch sunsets every day.
b.   Students <u>wanting to study abroad</u> are adventurous.
c.   Tickets <u>bought on the Internet</u> are cheaper.
d.   The books <u>on the table</u> are mine.

3.9.10 (page 163)
You can reduce the clause by omitting *who/which that* and *be:* Ex. 1) The keys (that are) on the key chain belong to me. Ex. 2) The kids (who are) playing in the room are cute. Ex. 3) The site (that was) chosen for the next Olympics is in Russia.

3.9.11 (page 163)
You can reduce the clause by omitting the relative pronoun and changing the verb to the *–ing* form) The kids (who play) in the room are smart; the kids playing in the room are smart. (NOTE: This rule applies only to active voice. In passive voice, we omit the relative pronoun and *be: The ship [that was] destroyed in the battle was relatively new* as discussed in 3.9.10.)

3.9.12 (page 164)
a. 3
b. 1 (OR: 4)
c. 4
d. 2
e. 1
f. 3
g. 2
h. 4
i. 4
j. 1 (OR: 4)
k. 3
l. 2

3.9.13 (page 165)
My family lives in an apartment <u>that</u> is not very big. The building which the apartment is located in has nine floors, and our apartment is on the eighth floor. It has three bedrooms, a kitchen, and a bathroom. The room <u>that</u> (or <u>which</u>) my sister and I share is smaller than the other two rooms. Our room has a bunk bed <u>which</u> (or <u>that</u>) saves a lot of space. Our parents have their own <u>room right</u> (or <u>room that is right</u> or <u>room which is right</u>) next to ours. Down the corridor, we have a living room <u>that</u> also serves as our dining room because it is located very close to the kitchen. The kitchen that my mom cooks <u>in</u> every day has a lot of plants. The apartment that <u>I</u> live in is nice, but I wish it were a bit bigger. The room <u>where my sister and I sleep</u> is too small.

Action Research (page 165): Answers will vary.

ELL Grammar Key 10: *Infinitives and Gerunds*
3.10.1 (page 166)
An infinitive consists of *to* plus the simple base form of a verb. It can function as a noun (Our decision was to go to a different restaurant), adjective (The best place to go is Korea), or adverb (We paid extra to go on an earlier flight).

3.10.2 (page 166)
Answers will vary. Possible answers include *to go, to play, to laugh, to sleep, to listen, to dance, to hug, to dream.*

3.10.3 (page 166)
A gerund consists of a VERB + *-ing.* It is always a noun.

3.10.4 (page 166)
Answers will vary. Possible answers include *going, playing, laughing, sleeping, listening, dancing, hugging, dreaming.*

3.10.5 (page 166)
Answers will vary. Possible answers include
a. Listening is important.
b. Swimming is my favorite sport.
c. Surfing scares me.
d. Arguing doesn't solve anything.
e. Running burns up a huge number of calories.

3.10.6 (page 166)
Infinitives can be a reduction of the phrase *in order to*. Notice a comma after this introductory phase. With introductory infinitive phrases meaning "in order to," the subject of the sentence appears after the comma.

3.10.7 (page 166)
It is determined by the preceding verb. ELLs should memorize which verbs are followed by infinitives and which by gerunds.

3.10.8 (page 167)
Followed by infinitives: *intend, hesitate, ask, want*; followed by gerunds: *dislike, be tired of, postpone, consider, think about*; followed by both: *hate, begin, start.*

3.10.9 (page 167)
Answers will vary. Possible answers include: I remember to brush my teeth, I remember visiting Cairo in 2005; I usually stop to watch the sunset, I stopped smoking many years ago; I always try to do my best, Try turning the knob to the left to turn on the radio; I forgot to charge my mobile, Have you forgotten talking to her?; I regret to inform you that you didn't win, I regret saying that.

3.10.10 (page 168)
After the word *need*, you use an infinitive. We never use *that* + subject + verb.

3.10.11 (page 168)
Answers will vary.

3.10.12 (page 168)
These verbs are usually followed by a person (noun or pronoun) and the base form of the verb. In addition, *help* may be followed by a person and an infinitive.

3.10.13 (page 168)
Answers will vary. Possible answers include:
a. Thank you for doing your homework.
b. She excels in helping companies that are in trouble.
c. I am in favor of traveling to the island.
d. We talked about going to the mall.

3.10.14 (page 169)
a. 3
b. 1
c. 2
d. 3
e. 1
f. 2
g. 1
h. 3
i. 2
j. 2
k. 3
l. 1

3.10.15 (page 170)
Playing in a casino is a kind of entertainment. There are lots of games to choose and play. When you win, you want to come back to play again and again. It is not even easy for highly paid professionals to get that kind of money to waste on gambling. People want to gamble to get high returns. However, this may be the beginning of an addiction. Many people become gamblers because they like to take risks, and they think that gambling is a quick and easy way to get lots of money in a short time. It is very easy to gamble because there are a lot of casinos where people can play any time they want.

Action Research (page 170): Answers will vary.

ELL Grammar Key 11: *Phrasal Verbs*

3.11.1 (page 171)
A phrasal verb is the combination of a verb and a particle (or a preposition or adverb) that creates a new meaning.

3.11.2 (page 171)
Answers will vary.

3.11.3 (page 171)
Phrasal verbs: a. e. f. verb + prepositional phrase: b. c. d.

3.11.4 (page 171)
Because ELLs do not know about the existence of phrasal verbs and often do not have phrasal verbs in their native languages. In addition, phrasal verbs are usually idiomatic.

3.11.5 (page 171)
Phrasal verbs are extremely common in English speaking and writing and often determine the meaning of the entire sentence.

3.11.6 (page 171)
They do not have phrasal verbs in their native languages. Thus, ELLs who speak Latin-based languages such as Spanish or French may use a single-word cognate from their native language. Most bilingual dictionaries provide one-word translations or list the one-word translations before phrasal verbs if they even include phrasal verbs as listings.

3.11.7 (page 172)
Answers will vary. Possible answers include:

a. call off

b. figure out

c. go off

d. find out

e. run into

f. put up with

g. pick up

h. let out (OR: get away)

i. call on

j. go on

k. turn up

l. get in

3.11.8 (page 172)
A separable phrasal verb can be separated when there is a noun object. When there is a pronoun object, it must be separated.

3.11.9 (page 172)
Answers will vary. An example is *She called off the meeting. She called the meeting off. She called it off.*

3.11.10 (page 172)
A non-separable phrasal verb is a phrasal verb + a particle that cannot be separated by an object.

3.11.11 (page 172)
Answers will vary. An example is *He came across his long-lost wallet. He came across it.*

3.11.12 (page 173)
Answers will vary. Possible answers are

b. be able to communicate with, enter, finish

c. write a check, be able to see or understand, kiss

d. clean or arrange, invent, compensate for

3.11.13 (page 173)
Answers will vary.

3.11.14 (page 173)
An intransitive phrasal verb never has an object. Answers will vary. An example is *I grew up in Louisianna.*

3.11.15 (page 174)
Answers will vary.

3.11.16 (page 174)
a. 1
b. 3
c. 2
d. 1
e. 3
f. 2
g. 4
h. 3
i. 1
j. 4
k. 2
l. 4

3.11.17 (page 175)
Registering for TOEFL (Test of English as a Foreign Language) is a relatively easy thing to do. First, you need to figure <u>out</u> which type of TOEFL to register for. If you want to sign <u>up</u> for the one offered at your school, then you will most likely be studying for a paper-based test. An Internet-based test (iBT) is offered in testing centers around the world, and you must come <u>up</u> with the fee to pay for it. To register for an iBT, you must fill <u>out</u> and mail <u>in</u> a form from the TOEFL Bulletin, call <u>up</u> the testing company, or go online. Once you have made your mind up about the test type, calm <u>down</u> and carefully prepare for it. If you fail, don't be afraid to do <u>it</u> <u>over</u>. You are not alone.

Action Research (page 175): Answers will vary.

ELL Grammar Key 12: *Modals*

3.12.1 (page 176)
A modal verb is an auxiliary, or helping verb, that alters the meaning of the sentence by adding shades of meaning, or mood, to the main verb that it modifies.

3.12.2 (page 176)
Answers will vary. Possible answers include *may, might, can could, will, would, shall, should,* and *must.*

3.12.3 (page 176)
a. ELLs' native languages may or may not have a direct translation for each modal.
b. Any modal can have multiple meanings that may overlap with those of another modal, which makes comprehension of modals more difficult.

3.12.4 (page 176)
a. ELLs try to conjugate modals.
b. ELLs try to follow modals with the infinitive form of a verb.
c. ELLs attempt to use the auxiliary *do* when negating and in questions.

3.12.5 (page 176)
Modals sometimes share meanings and can be confusing to ELLs. For example, *may* can mean possibility, but so can *might.*

3.12.6 (page 176)

Lower-proficiency students are learning modals as new words and need time to absorb this kind of information. Higher-proficiency students can consolidate their knowledge through a lesson that groups and ranks modals, for example, in terms of degrees of possibility.

3.12.7 (page 177)
Answers will vary.

3.12.8 (page 178)
Answers will vary.

3.12.9 (page 179)
a. 2
b. 1
c. 4
d. 2
e. 3
f. 5
g. 4
h. 5
i. 1
j. 2
k. 1
l. 3

3.12.10 (page 180)

My father always tells me that I will <u>achieve</u> great things if I study hard. I know that he <u>must be</u> right, but I am not sure what I want to do in life. I liked to build things when I was little, so engineering <u>could become</u> my career. My dad is an engineer. He can always <u>help</u> and guide me when I need his support. On the other hand, I <u>might consider</u> a career in accounting since I am good with money and finances. It <u>would be</u> convenient to go to school because one of the best business colleges in the state is next to my house. I am still not sure. I <u>should think</u> more about it, but one thing is for certain. I <u>can do</u> anything I want. This is great.

Action Research (page 180): Answers will vary.

ELL Grammar Key 13: *Word Forms*

3.13.1 (page 181)
a. ELLs will be able to recognize the part of the speech of a word by using its suffix. On seeing the word *payment*, ELLs can recognize it as a noun because of *–ment*.
b. ELLs will be able to produce correct forms of a given word by adding the correct suffix. To make the verb *pay* into a noun, ELLs know to produce *payment* instead of **payity* or **payation*.

3.13.2 (page 181)
interpretation, interpreter, interpretable, interpretive, interpreting, interpreted, interpretively; response, responder, responsive, —, responding, responded, responsively; creation, creator, creative, —, creating, created, creatively

3.13.3 (page 181)
va<u>ry</u>, vari<u>able</u>, variab<u>ly</u>, vari<u>ation</u> (or vari<u>ety</u>); conceptual<u>ize</u>, conceptual<u>ized</u>, conceptu<u>ally</u>, concept; institu<u>tionalize</u>, institution<u>al</u>, institution<u>ally</u>, insti<u>tution</u>; secure, secure, secure<u>ly</u>, secur<u>ity</u>; exclude, exclu<u>sive</u>, exclusive<u>ly</u>, exclu<u>sion</u> (or exclu<u>sivity</u>)

3.13.4 (page 182)
Answers will vary.

3.13.5 (page 182)
Answers will vary.

3.13.6 (page 183)
Answers will vary.

3.13.7 (page 183)
Answers will vary. Examples may include *fast, hard,* and *yesterday.*

3.13.8 (page 183)
Answers will vary. Examples may include *lovely* and *friendly.*

3.13.9 (page 183)
Answers will vary.

3.13.10 (page 184)
Answers will vary.

3.13.11 (page 185)
a. 1
b. 1
c. 3
d. 3
e. 1
f. 2
g. 2
h. 1
i. 1
j. 1
k. 3
l. 2

3.13.12 (page 186)
Grammar class is my favorite of all the classes I am taking this semester. There are only fifteen students in this class, and they come from six <u>different</u> countries. <u>Naturally,</u> we all have to speak English. The teacher is so <u>friendly.</u> She <u>explains</u> everything very well and always gives us the <u>answers</u> to the homework exercises. At the <u>beginning</u> of the semester, we received a <u>detailed</u> schedule, so we now know when we have tests and quizzes and when homework <u>assignments</u> are due. I am learning a lot in this class. I wish I could take more classes with the same teacher next semester.

Action Research (page 186): Answers will vary.

ELL Grammar Key 14: *Passive Voice*
3.14.1 (page 187)
Six detailed emails <u>were written</u> by Mary. This book <u>has been read</u> by chidren for almost a century. Our economy <u>will be affected</u> by the price of oil for the next decade. An arena <u>is being built</u> by three companies. The village <u>was destroyed</u> by a tornado.

3.14.2 (page 187)
A form of the verb *to be* (OR: *get*) and a past participle

3.14.3 (page 188)
An apple <u>is eaten</u> by Jane every day. An apple <u>is being eaten</u> by Jane now. An apple <u>has</u> already <u>been eaten</u> by Jane. An apple <u>is going to be eaten</u> by Jane soon. An apple <u>had been eaten</u> by Jane before work.

3.14.4 (page 188)
Bill drives the car. Bill is driving the car. Bill has driven the car. Bill drove the car. Bill was driving the car. Bill had driven the car. Bill will drive the car. Bill will have driven the car.

3.14.5 (page 189)
In active voice, the subject is the doer of the action of the verb. In passive voice, the subject is the receiver of the action of the verb.

3.14.6 (page 189)
Answers will vary. (Example: *Barbara bought a car last year.*)

3.14.7 (page 189)
Answers will vary. (Example: *A car was bought by Barbara last year.*)

3.14.8 (page 189)
Answers will vary.

3.14.9 (page 190)
An intransitive verb is a verb that cannot have an object (direct object).

3.14.10 (page 190)
Answers will vary. Possible answers include *die, occur, happen, lie, look, listen, wait.*

3.14.11 (page 190)
We use passive voice when we want to emphasize the person or thing that is receiving the action more than or instead of the agent.

3.14.12 (page 190)
The *by* + doer phrase should be used when the doer (agent) is important to the rest of the story, especially when the doer represents new information that is not commonly known.

3.14.13 (page 190)
He is married describes his current marital status, and *He got married* talks about an event or action. The word *get* is similar to *become;* it implies a change, which implies an event or action.

3.14.14 (page 190)
Answers will vary.

3.14.15 (page 191)
Some ELLs find these sentences confusing because the words *interested* and *interesting* are both adjectives from the same base word *interest.* Some ELLs do not understand the difference between *-ing* adjectives and *-ed* adjectives.

3.14.16 (page 191)
In general, we use the present participle *(-ing)* to describe the person or thing that is doing that action, and we use the past participle to describe the person or thing that receives the action. Therefore, we talk about *an interesting class* because the class is what causes the interest, and we talk about *an interested student* because the student receives the action of the class or teacher.

3.14.17 (page 191)
Answers will vary. Possible answers include
    The book was confusing. The students were confused.
    The movie was exciting. The audience members were excited.
    The mystery novel is puzzling. The readers are puzzled.

3.14.18 (page 192)
Three additional original answers per preposition will vary.

to	with	of	by
be accustomed to	be acquainted with	be ashamed of	be bored by
be committed to	be bored with	be composed of	be impressed by
be dedicated to	be disappointed with	be convinced of	be surprised by
be devoted to	be done with	be made of	
be married to	be fed up with	be scared of	
be opposed to	be finished with	be terrified of	
be related to	be impressed with	be tired of	
be used to	be satisfied with		

about	from	in	at
be confused about	be divorced from	be disappointed in	be surprised at
be excited about	be exhausted from	be dressed in	
be worried about	be made from	be interested in	
	be tired from		

3.14.19 (page 193)

a. 1
b. 2
c. 5
d. 3
e. 4
f. 1
g. 5
h. 2
i. 1
j. 3
k. 2
l. 4

3.14.20 (page 194)

When I was <u>working</u> as an engineer in Cali, Colombia, my company <u>was</u> awarded a multi-million dollar contract to build a new school. The project was closely <u>supervised</u> by the city officials, and tight deadlines <u>were</u> set. Therefore, we had to work quickly and efficiently. I was <u>assigned</u> as a project manager and <u>given</u> (or: <u>was given</u>) tasks that required me to be on site. The construction <u>was complicated</u> by constant rains. However, we managed to complete the school by the next academic year, and the company <u>was</u> chosen as one of the best engineering and construction companies in the country.

Action Research (page 194): Answers will vary.

ELL Grammar Key 15: *Conditionals* (If *Clauses*) *and* Wish

3.15.1 (page 195)

Sentence b is harder to understand. In Sentence a, the verb *took* is in past tense because the speaker is simply telling us past information. The action is past, and the verb form is past tense, so this is logical. In Sentence b, however, the verb form *took* appears to be talking about a past event, but here it is referring to a present action. The tense and the time of *took the test* do not match in Sentence b.

3.15.2 (page 195)

This sentence is difficult because the verb forms are not the usual ones used. Past perfect *(had known)* is usually used for the older of two past actions, but this action did not happen, so some ELLs may wonder why past perfect tense is used here. In the phrase *I would have stopped by*, it actually sounds like the action happened when in fact the action did not happen. In addition, the reduced (contracted) forms are hard to hear and comprehend.

3.15.3 (page 195)
A conditional sentence expresses actions that did not happen, are not happening, or will not happen unless a certain condition is met.

3.15.4 (page 195)
Answers will vary.

3.15.5 (page 195)
A conditional sentence has two parts: a main clause (an independent clause) and a condition (a dependent clause). When the main clause is followed by a condition, no comma is necessary. However, when the condition comes first, it must be followed by a comma.

3.15.6 (page 196)
Answers will vary.

3.15.7 (page 196)
Answers will vary.

3.15.8 (page 196)
if clause: simple present, present progressive, present perfect, present perfect progressive; result clause: will, be going to, any modal

3.15.9 (page 197)
Answers will vary.

3.15.10 (page 197)
if clause: simple past, past progressive; result clause: *would, could, might*

3.15.11 (page 197)
Answers will vary.

3.15.12 (page 197)
If clause: past perfect, past perfect progressive; result clause: *would have* + past particple, *may/might/could have* + past participle

3.15.13 (page 198)
Answers will vary.

3.15.14 (page 198)
In most conditional sentences, the verb in the main clause and the verb in the condition are both talking about the same time (past, present, or future). In a mixed conditional, the two sentence parts are referring to different times, such as a present main result clause with a past condition.

3.15.15 (page 198)
Answers will vary. A possible answer is: *If I had eaten eariler, I would not be hungry now.*

3.15.16 (page 198)
It is possible to omit *if* in a conditional sentence when the *if* clause contains the words *were*, *had*, or *should*. In this case, question word order must be used.

3.15.17 (page 198)
Both sentences sound like they are describing past events that actually happened. In reality, however, only Sentence a is describing a past fact. In Sentence b, the small word *if* is crucial to understanding that neither of the verb phrases in that sentence is talking about a real occurrence.

3.15.18 (page 199)
Sentences with *wish* are similar in meaning to unreal conditions in the present, future, or past. The situation is not true, does not exist, is unlikely to happen, or did not happen. To wish about a past action, we use past perfect tense (instead of simple past). To wish about a present situation, we use past tense (instead of present tense). To wish about a future event, *will* changes to *would*. The verb after the word *wish* is often in a tense that is one time period earlier than the actual time of the action.

3.15.19 (page 199)

a. 3	g. 1
b. 1	h. 2
c. 2	i. 3
d. 4	j. 1
e. 3	k. 1
f. 2	l. 4

3.15.20 (page 200)
I am studying English in the U.S. right now, but I wish I <u>were</u> back home in Korea so that I could eat my mom's food every day. She makes the best bibimpab, stir fried vegetables with rice and beef. If I <u>had known</u> that I <u>would</u> miss her cooking so much, I would <u>have paid</u> more attention when she was cooking. Food here is different. It is hard to find the right ingredients. I wish I <u>had</u> an Asian supermarket next to my house. If it <u>were</u> closer, I <u>could</u> go shopping there more often. I wish I <u>had</u> some Korean food right now.

Action Research (page 200): Answers will vary.

Chapter 4 (pages 201–208)

1. See HB pp. 266–267.	11. See HB p. 277.
2. See HB pp. 267–268.	12. See HB pp. 277–278.
3. See HB pp. 268–269.	13. See HB pp. 278–279.
4. See HB pp. 269–270.	14. See HB p. 279.
5. See HB pp. 270–271.	15. See HB pp. 280–281.
6. See HB pp. 271–272.	16. See HB pp. 281–282.
7. See HB pp. 272–273.	17. See HB pp. 282–283.
8. See HB pp. 273–274.	18. See HB pp. 283–284.
9. See HB p. 274.	19. See HB pp. 284–285.
10. See HB pp. 275–276.	20. See HB p. 286.

Chapter 5 (pages 209–214)

Exercise 5.1 (pages 209–212)
Answers will vary.

Exercise 5.2 (pages 213–214)
Answers will vary.